Break Up, Don't Crack Up

Disclaimer

While every care has been taken in the production of this book, no legal responsibility is accepted, warranted or implied by the author, editor or publisher in respect of any errors, omissions or mis-statements. You should always seek professional or legal advice from a suitably qualified person when appropriate.

Break Up, Don't Crack Up

*A Positive Plan for your
Separation or Divorce in Ireland*

Rachel Fehily

ORPEN PRESS

Orpen Press
Lonsdale House
Avoca Avenue
Blackrock
Co. Dublin
Ireland

e-mail: info@orpenpress.com
www.orpenpress.com

Paperback ISBN 978-1-871305-32-6
ePub ISBN 978-1-871305-50-0
Kindle ISBN 978-1-871305-51-7

Printed in the UK by MPG Ltd.

This book is dedicated to everyone who is going through a difficult separation or divorce

About the Author

Rachel Fehily is an author, barrister and mediator with over sixteen years of experience. She runs a mediation and dispute resolution service for individuals, couples and families who are experiencing conflict before, during and after relationship breakdown, divorce, separation or family law litigation. She contributes widely to the national media on the subjects of relationship breakdown and conflict resolution. She is the author of *Split: True Stories of Relationship Breakdown in Ireland*.

Acknowledgements

I would like to thank the following people for their friendship, help and encouragement:

Mr Richard Bennett, Ms Judy Blake, BL, Ms Rhona Boylan, Ms Nuala Butler, SC, Ms Patricia Bunyan, Mr Pierre and Mrs Tanya Chapeau, Ms Tina Christiansen, Ms Lana Citron, Mr Jack Cosgrave, Mr Aidan Cosgrave, Ms Juliet Cronin, Ms Rachel Dalton, Mr Robert Doran, Ms Emily Egan, SC, Prof. James and Mrs Margaret Fehily, Mr John Fehily, Mr Eric Fehily, Mrs Natalie Dion-Fehily, Ms Jane Fehily, Mr Christian Fehily, Mr Ben and Mrs Jennifer Fehily, Mr Morgan Fehily, Ms Totti Fehily, Dr Max and Dr Anne Fehily, Mr David Foley, Dr Michael Gibson, Mr Eugene Gleeson, Mr Harvey Gleeson, Mrs Jennifer Gordon-Yusko, Prof. David and Mrs Pam Harris, Mr Charlie and Mrs Sue Harvey, Mr Niall Hill, BL, Mrs Laura Hogan, Ms Penny Iremonger, Mr Declan Keaveney, Mrs Victoria Larson Kavanagh, Mrs Mary Kelly, Ms Chenile Keogh, Ms Lijana Kuklyte, Mr Tom and Mrs Catherine Lenehan, Mr Toby McArdle, Ms Jackie McCarthy, Ms Aileen Lennon, Mr Conor Mackey, Mr James Mackey, Mrs Mimi Shiel, Mr John McKeon, Mr John and Mrs Sarah Murphy, Mr Benji Murphy, Ms Stephanie Murphy, Mr Ross Murphy, Ms Cliona O'Brien, Ms Helene O'Brien, Ms Slaney O'Brien, Mr William and Mrs Carmel O'Grady, Dr John O'Grady, Ms Aisling O'Kelly, BL, Ms Carla O'Kelly, Ms Imogen O'Kelly,

Acknowledgements

Mrs Lucy O'Kelly, Mr Mark O'Mahony, BL, Ms Avril O'Riordan, Mr Luigi Rea, BL, Ms Aideen Ryan, Mr Daragh Scaife, Ms Donna Seagal, Ms Emma Weir, Ms Iseult White, Mr Kieron Wood, BL and Mr Ed Yusko.

I would also like to thank the staff at Orpen Press, Elizabeth Brennan and Nuala O'Reilly for their invaluable input into every aspect of this book. I would especially like to thank Eileen O'Brien at Orpen Press for her suggestions, patience, creativity and intelligent and meticulous editing of this book and Dr John Bowman, broadcaster and historian, for his invaluable advice and for generously sharing his extensive knowledge of writing and publishing with me.

Contents

Preface xiii

1. Organising Yourself 1
   Introduction 1
   Breaking the news 4
   Looking after your health 9
   Therapy, counselling and advice 13
   Learning conflict resolution skills 23
   Making a list 26

2. Putting Children First 29
   Being a good parent 29
   Your child's rights 35
   Your child's financial security and maintenance ... 39
   Guardianship, custody and access 47
   Making a parenting plan 52
   Your child's emotional well-being 62

3. Alternative Dispute Resolution 69
   Introduction 69
   The best conditions for ADR 73
   ADR in Ireland 79
   Mediation 82
   Collaborative law 89
   Counselling 94

4. **Lawyers and Litigation** **99**
   Introduction 99
   Your family law case 103
   The Legal Aid Board 113
   Hiring a lawyer 116
   Representing yourself 119
   Interacting with your lawyer 122
   Controlling your costs 124

5. **Managing Your Finances** **131**
   Introduction 131
   Untangling your finances 134
   Civil partnership and cohabitation under the
      new 2010 Act 138
   What do the courts do? 140
   Maintenance 146
   Dividing your joint assets 147
   Bankruptcy, mortgages and debt management 159
   Budgeting 163
   Living on less 165

6. **Other Issues** **167**
   Domestic violence 167
   Child abuse 174
   False accusations 176
   Parental child abduction 178
   Lesbian, gay, bisexual and transgender issues 183
   Annulment of your marriage or civil partnership. 186

7. **Your New Life** **191**
   Your new circle 191
   Behaving well 193
   New partners and step-parenting 198
   New friends and dating 203

Contents

Conclusion **213**

Further Reading **215**

Resources **221**

Preface

'Knowledge is power.' – *Sir Francis Bacon*

If you are upset because your relationship has just broken down or you're in the middle of trying to deal with your break-up then you need help. After a relationship ends there are usually lots of important decisions to make. You may have to decide how to tell your children about the break-up, how to parent apart, whether to hire a lawyer and what to do about your dwindling finances.

Making those decisions when you are suffering emotionally isn't easy. People who are in the middle of a break-up often take action without taking time, gathering information and getting the best possible advice from the experts.

I wrote *Break Up, Don't Crack Up: A Positive Plan for your Separation or Divorce in Ireland* because I think it helps to get as much information and practical advice as you can before you take action and make those important decisions.

It doesn't matter if you are a same sex or an opposite sex couple, with or without children; everyone faces a tough time when it comes to dealing with the fallout of their relationship breakdown. You will need to focus wisely on what action you should take so that you can ensure the best possible outcome for your family, friends and wider social circle.

Practicing as a barrister and a mediator has given me a broad experience of conflict resolution. I drew on my experience when I wrote this book. As a mediator I have been able to help people to think strategically about how to deal with their relationship breakdown and take a holistic approach to solving their problems. I think that different problems need different responses and when you're experiencing relationship breakdown it's crucial that you go to the right expert and get the right advice for your particular problem.

In Ireland we have an adversarial family law system, so your lawyer is there to negotiate on your behalf and fight your corner. Lawyers don't always have the time to give their clients all the help and support they need. The emotions that people experience when their relationships break down are similar to a bereavement, only it's worse because the person they loved is still alive but the relationship is not.

Hiring a lawyer is useful and often necessary but it doesn't always help people to sort out the underlying stresses that are in their lives and their relationships. If things are getting on top of you it's okay to admit it, and go to your GP for help or find a good counsellor who will listen to you.

Mediation is a form of dispute resolution that takes place outside the courtroom where a neutral third party will assist you to negotiate or help you think creatively about how to resolve your issues after relationship breakdown. It's always worth trying mediation assisted by legal advice because if it works it can save you time and money, reduce trauma for you and your family and break the cycle of conflict that can ensue after a relationship breaks down.

Break Up, Don't Crack Up should be read chronologically because it starts with looking after yourself. If you're not in good shape mentally and physically you won't be able to think clearly, gather and analyse information, and make the best decisions. It goes on to explain the importance of putting children first in Chapter 2 and then advises you on how to use alternative dispute resolution and the ins and outs of lawyers and litigation in Chapters 3 and 4. Chapter 5 helps you with the problem of managing your finances, and Chapter 6 deals with other issues that may arise. Finally, Chapter 7 gives you information on how to move on with your new life when the dust has settled.

Take the time to read the information in this book and use the resources and further reading to find out as much as you can before you make those crucial decisions about how to approach the fallout from your relationship breakdown.

Use the six-step plan:

1. I will look after myself.
2. I will put my children first.
3. If possible, I will try alternative dispute resolution.
4. If I have to litigate, I will litigate well.
5. I will not neglect my finances.
6. I will move on to my new life without bitterness and regret.

1

Organising Yourself

*Introduction – Breaking the news – Looking after your health –
Therapy, counselling and advice – Learning conflict resolution skills
– Making a list*

Introduction

Human beings have a social, cultural and biological drive
to love and want to be loved in return. They give and
receive love through their relationships with their children, spouses, partners, family and friends. Ireland is a
developed country and most of us don't struggle with
starvation and disease on a daily basis. For that reason,
Irish men and women have the time to nurture their relationships and put them at the centre of their emotional
lives. It can be devastating when these relationships don't
work out and whether you are married, in a civil partnership, recognised by law as cohabitants, sharing a house or
living together with your children, you are a family and
your relationship is central to your lives. For many, the
end of their familial relationship in one of the most traumatic things they will ever experience.

No one is immune from the complications, pain and
conflict that ensue post break-up; like death, it is a great

leveller. Hollywood actors, rock stars, royalty, politicians and billionaires all face the same difficulties as you and your family. They try to publicly deal with their grief, negotiate with an uncooperative ex and nervously go to court and fight over shared parenting and the division of assets.

Life can be unbearable; you are trying to accept that your partner or spouse no longer loves you and has started a relationship with someone else or you may be feeling desperately guilty for leaving. Trying to look after children, missing your children, feeling depressed and suffering financially – it becomes a crazy, dramatic roller-coaster, with suffering and sadness all around.

Relationship break-ups are a common human experience and they can be a positive life lesson, a tragedy or something in between. We all know a co-worker, friend or family member who has experienced a break-up horror. The things that made their break-up sad or difficult are different from the things that turned it into a long-running soap opera.

The initial feelings of anger, shock, betrayal, loss and grief are normal when a person you love exits your life and there is no way around that pain. Like every loss you have to go through it, experience it and it will fade with time. Hopefully you will come out the other side wiser, more experienced and in a better frame of mind.

After the actual break-up 'event', post break-up difficulties that drag on and seem never-ending are caused by continuing conflict around issues that need to be resolved between you and your ex. Many issues can arise and do arise, but the main areas of conflict are usually focused around parenting and the division of assets.

The initial pain is personal to you, and you ought to get all the help and support you can to minimise the hurt and speed up your recovery. The joint issues you have to resolve and continue to communicate about with your ex are easier to deal with if you are in good physical and mental shape.

The aim of this first chapter is to help you to organise and look after yourself post break-up. It is not about looking after other people or trying to resolve the almost inevitable conflict that will arise over parenting and financial matters. It is about preparing yourself and getting into a strong frame of mind so that you will be able to cope with what lies ahead.

Obviously your children come first, and good parents will put their children's needs ahead of their own. The second chapter is about looking after your children and you can read Chapters 1 and 2 together. The reason the chapter about looking after yourself comes first is because it's impossible for a person to deal with parenting, financial issues and conflict if they are not functioning well.

The other chapters in the book provide information that will help you plan how to deal with various other issues that arise post break-up. Chapter 3 looks at the different types of dispute resolution methods that are available in Ireland. Chapter 4 gives you guidance on how to hire a lawyer and work through the legal system if you have to go down that route.

Chapter 5 is about managing your finances post break-up and Chapter 6 covers some of the other issues that arise during break-ups. Chapter 7 looks at your life post break-up and gives information on how to handle conflict within your new circle, extended family and friends after the dust has settled. It also gives you some tips on meeting new people and taking the plunge into the dating scene again.

But before you start feeling overwhelmed by the thought of making decisions about parenting and living arrangements, finances and long-term plans you also need to make sure that your health is okay and you're in the right state of mind to make those important decisions.

You or the people close to you, including your children, may need therapy, counselling or advice and this chapter explains what's available in Ireland and the differences between the various therapies. The end of the chapter offers advice on conflict resolution skills that may help you deal with conflict as it arises.

Breaking the News

Breaking the News to your Partner or Spouse

It's very important to think about how you communicate at the time of the end of your relationship with your ex- or soon-to-be ex-partner or spouse and the manner in which news of the break-up is told to your family and friends. Simultaneously you must look after yourself emotionally and physically so that you are in good shape to face the fallout after your break-up.

The lead-up to the end of your relationship and the immediate aftermath of a break-up is a critical time for you. Be sure that you have exhausted all avenues, whether it's counselling or help from other sources, before you make that final decision. Divorce and separation is the most upsetting thing that can happen in your and your children's lives, next to the death of someone you love, so when you decide to end your relationship don't do so lightly.

If you are the person who is about to end the relationship, please think carefully about how you are going to do it. If you are leaving your partner or spouse because you're unhappy with the relationship or you've met someone else you ought to be as careful as you can be in how you break the news.

4

If you're seeing someone else and planning to l[...]
make sure you tell your partner or spouse before the[...]
find out for themselves. Hearing the news in a controlled
manner is better than reading it in an indiscreet email or
text message or hearing it from a third party. Ireland is a
tiny country and it's very easy to get found out, so as soon
as you're sure the relationship is over break the news as
sensitively and tactfully as you can.

Give your partner or spouse some respect in the manner
in which you tell them the relationship is over. Don't leave
suddenly without any warning or communicate by phone
or text – this is cruel and disrespectful. Unless you're seriously worried about abuse or violence you should try to
sit down face to face and explain why you are ending the
relationship in a calm, clear and compassionate manner.
Be prepared to listen to a certain amount of anger and
verbal abuse but put a limit on it. Whatever you do, don't
get angry.

If you're ending the relationship for other reasons make
sure you explain the reason clearly and sensitively. Your
ex may have problems with alcohol, drugs or fidelity. You
may have fallen out of love because of lack of communication, mistrust, family issues, dishonesty or a roving eye.
The chances are these issues have been discussed already
so they won't come as a complete surprise.

If you have children don't involve them in the meeting
with your spouse or partner. The break-up is about your
relationship, not about them. The ideal situation would be
if you and your ex could sit down and tell the children
together in a calm and controlled manner that your relationship has ended and you both are still there for them
and are prepared to work hard as parents to minimise the
effect of the break-up on them.

ed the relationship with you then you
e to plan your reaction. Seek help and
end or family member as soon as you
e children try to control your expression
. Having a meltdown in front of your
chilaic.. g them intimate details of the reason you
and their other parent are breaking up is not a good idea;
you will regret the hurt it causes them and the damage it
does to their relationship with you both.

Breaking the News to your Children

Some couples separate amicably or are on talking terms
when it comes to telling the news of the break-up to their
children. If this applies to you, and you have time to plan
it in advance, a joint meeting with the children is ideal. If
it can't be a joint meeting, you ought to meet with them
on your own and explain everything in the same manner.

The points you need to keep in mind and express clearly
to your children in an age appropriate manner when you
break the news are:

- Be honest with your children up to a point. Explain
  simply that you are both not happy living together
  and that you need to live in different homes. You don't
  need to show your anger or tell them details that are
  only appropriate for adults.

- Tell the children that you both love them very much
  and the separation has nothing to do with them, that
  you are always very happy with them and their behaviour didn't cause the break-up.

- Next you should explain any changes that are going
  to take place in living arrangements. Answer all the

questions your children have openly and honestly. If you don't know what's going to happen over the next few months explain that you will make a parenting plan that will cover everything they are concerned about.

- Again you should reassure your children and let them know that they will continue to see both of you as much as possible, that you both love them very much and they are in no way responsible for your break-up.

After breaking the news to your ex and your children you or your ex will probably leave the family home. You may have arranged alternative accommodation or your ex may decide to go somewhere temporarily until arrangements can be made. Leaving is usually the best thing to do as staying will only cause the conversation to continue for days rather than hours. If you're worried about your ex's emotional well-being you might have to stay or make sure a friend or family member is on the way so that you don't leave them on their own.

Allow the children to see where their other parent has gone to live as soon as possible. It's better for them if they go to visit their parent in their new home the next day so they can see where he or she is located. It's much less upsetting for children to see what's actually happening rather than letting their imaginations take over.

Breaking the News to your Family and Friends

After you've told the news to your ex and your children you will have to think about how to break the news to your family and friends. You ought to tell the people you are closest to (your family or very good friends) first as they should be the most supportive. If you are separating amicably you might break the news to your family together but normally you will be telling your family and your ex will tell his or her family. It's best not to give too much information initially as there is always the chance that you might get back together again. If you give too much information you might shock your family or friends and change their attitude towards both of you.

You may be surprised by the reaction of your family and friends. If they are very close to your ex they will be upset and have divided loyalties. They may want to maintain contact with your ex and this can be difficult to accept. If they never liked your ex or thought he or she was abusive then they may be relieved that the relationship is over. Either way you should not see their reaction as a reflection on you – it is their expression of their feelings about your ex.

If you break up because you've caught your ex being unfaithful or because he or she has been abusive or is exhibiting addictive behaviour it might be tempting to tell his or her family as an act of revenge, especially if you are close to your in-laws. Be careful about this because you may force your ex's family to take sides against you or your ex and this can cause both families and their in-laws to become polarised. It's important to clear up misunderstandings or lies if it becomes apparent that you are being badmouthed, but it's good to hold back from going into all the details until you are calmer and some time has passed. It may not be to your or your children's advantage to have every detail of your break-up immediately shared with both your families. Perhaps there are things from your past that you wouldn't like your ex to share with your parents, so even though it is difficult be careful not to overshare at this time.

Your close friends should be supportive of you and they may not be surprised if your relationship has been rocky for some time. As a couple you will have made friends with other couples and your break-up will cause you to re-evaluate the people who are in your life. Inevitably you will lose some of your joint friends and you ought not to see that as a reflection on you. Your real friends will stay with you and the ones who fade away were acquaintances or convenient friends.

Looking after Your Health

Post break-up it's normal to feel at a low emotionally and physically and it's often difficult to separate the two areas. Medical practitioners acknowledge that many of our physical ailments are inextricably linked to our mental outlook and that our mental outlook can be affected by our physical ailments. Our mind and body interact and affect each other whether we are aware of it or not.

It's normal to feel bad for a while, but if you're worried or your symptoms are lasting a long time you should get yourself checked out by your general practitioner (GP). In Ireland GPs are at the frontline of medical care. Many of them are excellent and have a wealth of expertise and experience. People build up a relationship with their local GP and go to them to discuss and be treated for a vast range of medical and personal problems. Don't be embarrassed to discuss the effect of your break-up on your mental and physical health with your GP; he or she will have heard anything you have to say many times before.

GPs come across upset, depression and anxiety every single day and they should be able to help you. Even the act of telling your GP how you're feeling can cause you to realise how affected you are emotionally. People burst into tears in front of their GPs all the time so, if that happens, don't be worried about it; it doesn't mean your GP will think you're having a breakdown. If your GP thinks you need counselling or medication they will refer you to another professional or prescribe some medication for you.

You may have a whole range of symptoms you need to discuss with your GP. It's best to write down the things you're concerned about before you go for your appointment. If you have a lot of things you want to discuss and it's a busy practice ask for a longer appointment. If you haven't had a check-up in a while and want to get a general health check you will probably need to get a range of blood tests. Ask your GP's secretary if you need to come in fasting if you're planning on getting blood tests.

Some of your symptoms may be stress related. You might be experiencing aches and pains, muscle spasms, panic attacks, sleep disturbance, heart palpitations, mood swings and tiredness. The problem with these symptoms is that they may not be stress related – you might have a problem with your blood pressure, an upset stomach, low iron levels, thyroid imbalances or an underlying illness or virus. It's difficult to know the cause of many symptoms but a good GP will work it out for you or send you to a specialist if necessary.

If you've been to your GP and ruled out physical illness or depression and you're still feeling low there are a few obvious things that you can do to make yourself feel better; your GP or a good therapist will recommend them to you. Here is a list of things that can help when you're feeling down and they definitely can't harm you.

Allow Yourself Grieving Time and then Set a Date

If you're obsessing about your ex and grieving for the end of your relationship allow yourself a period of time to feel very sad and cry as much as you want to. It's normal to look back and think about what might have been. You have suffered a huge loss and need to adjust your whole world view.

If you are distraught, it's important to move on from that stage and the best thing to do is to set yourself a date for the end of your mourning period. Decide to do something symbolic or different for yourself on that date (you might start to socialise with some friends again). Make that the time when you try to stop your serious mourning period and start to look forward to your new post break-up life.

Improve your Sleep

Make sure you have what sleep experts call 'good sleep hygiene': if you don't get good quality sleep everything will get on top of you and you won't be able to cope. Good sleep hygiene sounds drastic but it can help; here is what the experts say you should do to get a good night's sleep:

- Remove all stimulants from your bedroom – TV, books and computers.

- Stop worrying about how many hours sleep you're getting. Lying down and relaxing is beneficial to you.

- Turn off the light at the same time every night; get into a routine.

- Don't lie in bed worrying about a particular problem. Go into another room and write down whatever's bothering you on a piece of paper and leave it there.

- Do yoga, meditation, breathing or relaxation exercises to wind down.

Increase your Exercise

Exercise is essential to your general well-being and is known to be great for warding off depression. If you can't afford to go to a gym it doesn't matter: walking and jogging are free. Irish people have become much more exercise conscious in the past twenty years. There are lots of gyms, clubs, and individual and group sporting activities and it's not expensive to participate. The public parks and local community centres have plenty of things going on all year round and there are many reasonably priced exercise classes available in every locality. You're sure to find something to suit your interests.

Get in Touch with Nature

Take your dog, children or friends for a walk. If you have children bring them hiking in the countryside. In Ireland we are lucky because the country is so small you're always near a mountain, park, forest or beach. Even if you live in the centre of Dublin, Cork or Galway you're never far from spectacular scenery – so get out there and watch the sun set or get up early and see a sunrise. Find a forest or hill to explore; you can take your camera with you and photograph the sky and the stars. Regularly getting in touch with nature is good for your head and your heart.

Mind your Relationships

Don't let your relationships slide. Now is not a good time to be on your own. If your relationship with your partner had been difficult in the time leading up to the actual break-up you may have lost touch with lots of people. Call up your family and friends, get in contact, tell them what's going on, invite them over to keep you company and, if it's offered, accept their help and support.

Alcohol, Food, Cigarettes or Worse

There's always a temptation to reach for your comfort blanket in times of crisis. If you find solace in alcohol, food, cigarettes or other substances be very careful. Hangovers are worse when you're down. A huge number of suicides occur when people are hung over or coming off a drugs binge, so if you feel bad without a hangover you're going to feel immeasurably worse with one.

Don't inflict it on yourself if you can't handle it. No one feels good after overindulging in bad food or smoking too much, so give it a rest. Make yourself nice meals that you enjoy. Cook your favourite dinner with a glass or two of fantastic wine and a good dessert rather than stuffing your face with a box of chocolates or drinking a bottle of vodka; you won't feel so bad or so fat afterwards.

Therapy, Counselling and Advice

This section is about the different types of therapy, counselling and advice that are available. The information covers help for you but can also be read as an information source for your ex, children and extended family. Knowing what help can be sought and how to access it is important for everyone.

In Ireland, if you or someone close to you is suffering emotionally there are many, many different types of therapy, counselling and advice available. Your GP is a good first port of call and he or she is probably in the best position to advise you as to what type of counselling or therapy you might need. Counselling and therapy are unregulated in Ireland so you ought to understand the qualifications of the person treating you, and make sure they are, at the very least, a member of a regulated, professional body.

If your relationship has ended because you or your ex had an alcohol, drug, gambling or other addiction then you ought to discuss this with your GP. There are many different organisations that help with addictions and a break-up can sometimes give you or your ex the impetus to think about addiction.

Generally men outnumber women in reported substance abuse and suicide attempts and the recent increase in suicide numbers has been linked to the economic downturn. Women outnumber men in reported incidents of depression. Experts note that men in Ireland find it difficult to express themselves and it's not considered masculine in our culture to seek help. Men and women should never be ashamed to admit they have a problem and seek the appropriate help.

People who are suffering need to lose the shame they have about feeling depressed or suffering from a mental illness. As a society we need to treat mental illness like any other illness, and help someone who has a problem like depression in the same way as we would help them if they had a physical illness like cancer or a heart attack.

If you suspect you are depressed or need to talk to someone you may decide to make an appointment with a therapist off your own bat or your GP may refer you or suggest you make an appointment with a particular psychiatrist, psychologist, psychotherapist, cognitive behavioural therapist, addiction counsellor or other type of therapist. The following is a brief explanation of the differences between the various types of therapists and a description of the therapies they have to offer.

Psychiatrists

A psychiatrist is a doctor who has studied medicine and specialises in treating patients who have mental disorders. He or she will look at your problem from its physical, emotional and social perspectives and can prescribe medication, conduct a physical examination and order and interpret tests.

Psychiatrists often specialise in treating people of different ages (such as children, adolescents or geriatrics) or with specific illnesses or problems such as schizophrenia, psychosis, depression, eating disorders, personality disorders, gender identity disorders or addictions. Nowadays many people with mild mental disorders don't go to psychiatrists and disorders such as depression and anxiety are treated with medication by GPs. If you are suffering from suicidal thoughts, severe depression, mental illness or psychosis that has become acute post break-up your GP should refer you to a psychiatrist for a more expert diagnosis or management of your illness.

You will normally be put in contact with a psychiatrist in the public psychiatric services by GP referral. You will probably be put on a waiting list and receive an outpatient appointment for assessment. If you check into a hospital with acute symptoms and a psychiatrist is available you will be assessed in the emergency department of a hospital. If you want to be seen privately you can ask your GP for a referral letter and the name of a psychiatrist in private practice.

Psychiatrists work with other professionals such as psychologists, psychiatric nurses, occupational therapists and social workers as part of a multi-disciplinary team. They should work together, discuss your case and design a care plan that offers you support and help if you are suffering from an acute mental illness.

Psychologists

Psychologists usually study psychology in university and then go on to work as counsellors, therapists, academics or in research. Psychology is not regulated by law in Ireland but there is a register of psychologists maintained by the Psychological Society of Ireland which sets standards of practice and has a code of conduct and a complaints procedure for its members.

Psychologists don't prescribe medication so in order to help patients they engage them in 'talk therapy'. Many counselling psychologists study psychotherapy or cognitive behavioural therapy or follow a method or various methods of treatment based on their study and training.

Psychotherapists and Cognitive Behavioural Therapists

Psychotherapists

Psychotherapists may or may not have studied psychology. Psychotherapy has existed since the time of ancient Greece. Psychotherapists don't prescribe medication; they use 'talk therapy' – a structured professional relationship that allows the patient to disclose his or her feelings and thoughts to the therapist. The relationship is based on the therapist helping the patient to make changes in their life that will help them.

Cognitive Behavioural Therapists

Cognitive behavioural therapy (CBT) is a type of psychotherapy that is becoming increasing popular. It evolved in the 1980s and is based on the theory that our thoughts affect our emotions and our emotions affect our behaviour. Our brains sometimes can't distinguish between correct and dysfunctional thinking so we need to analyse our thoughts and replace our dysfunctional thinking with positive thoughts.

The focus of CBT is to help patients solve their problems with dysfunctional behaviour and cognition by using specific techniques to help, such as keeping a diary of their emotions and reactions, analysing their thoughts, gradually exposing themselves to activities they avoid, relaxation and mindfulness.

Accreditation Bodies

There are many accreditation bodies for psychotherapists and cognitive behavioural therapists and other types of therapists in Ireland and the UK. These associations are usually established to maintain standards, regulate training, and provide a complaints procedure and a code of practice for patients and practitioners.

These accrediting bodies include the Irish Association for Counselling and Psychotherapy (IACP), which has 3,250 members; the Irish Association of Humanistic and Integrative Psychotherapy (IAHIP), which has 600 members; the Association for Psychoanalysis and Psychotherapy in Ireland (APPI), which was set up in 1993 as an informal society mainly for graduates of the Masters programme in Clinical Psychotherapy at St Vincent's Hospital; and the Irish Association for Psychotherapy in Primary Care (IAPP), which accredits psychotherapists working in primary care.

Mental Health Organisations

The College of Psychiatry

In Ireland the psychiatric profession is regulated by the College of Psychiatry in Ireland and psychiatrists have to complete seven years of post-graduate training to become fully qualified psychiatrists.

The Mental Health Commission

The Mental Health Commission was established under the Mental Health Act 2001. It is an independent body set up to promote high standards in the delivery of mental health services and to protect the interests of patients who are detained involuntarily; these patients can be assigned lawyers by the Commission to represent their interests if necessary.

Young people who are inpatients in Irish psychiatric facilities or who suffer from mental disabilities are also protected by the Commission and can use the 'Headspace' tool kit, a self-advocacy and rights-based toolkit for young people who are availing of inpatient mental health services. The toolkit provides young people with information on what to expect in hospital and what their rights are. The Commission has developed a website version of the toolkit at www.headspaceireland.ie.

See Change

See Change is another important organisation – it acts as Ireland's national mental health stigma reduction partnership. It's made up of a coalition of organisations including the Department of Health, the Health Service Executive (HSE), the Mental Health Commission, St Patrick's University Hospital and the College of Psychiatry of Ireland. It's focused on the reduction of stigma and is working to challenge the discrimination faced by people who suffer from mental health problems.

Headstrong

Headstrong is another organisation that was set up to change the way Ireland thinks about youth mental health and to help young people stay connected to their community through research, advocacy and the development of their 'Jigsaw' model of community involvement. Jigsaw is a network of projects across Ireland that work with communities to support young people's health and wellbeing. It engages young people, organisations, families and other support agencies in communities so that they are better able to respond to the needs of young people aged 12 to 25.

Therapeutic Approaches

Talk therapy and cognitive behavioural therapy are the main approaches taken by psychologists and psychotherapists but there are hundreds of other different types of approaches. Different therapists follow different schools of thought and methodologies and many people find relief from alternative therapies.

Acupuncture, Chinese medicine, homeopathy, Ayurvedic medicine, reflexology and other therapies have been used by other cultures and in other countries for hundreds or thousands of years and many of their medicines and remedies are stocked in pharmacies and are covered by health insurers. However, it is important to use conventional medicine first before you engage in an alternative. There is no point in being treated for the symptoms of a serious illness with a medication or treatment that has no proven efficacy. At the same time, it's important that you have trust and confidence in your therapist and that your therapy works for you. No one can pass judgement on what works and what doesn't work for you personally. Sometimes the belief that a treatment works can cause you to feel better.

Unfortunately there is always the danger that you may be exploited at a vulnerable time in your life by a therapist who is not doing you any good. People who are intelligent, sensible and well-respected in the context of their work or private life can become prey to therapists who offer treatments that have no scientific basis and may even cause damage or distress.

As therapy in Ireland is unregulated you will find a huge range and choice of types of therapy to choose from. There are literally hundreds of different approaches to therapy and it's up to you to decide what works for you. If you want to, you can avail of Freudian or Gestalt therapy, existential psychotherapy, Jungian psychotherapy, Adlerian psychology, dialectical behaviour therapy, the Rubenfeld synergy method, somatic therapy, homeopathic therapy, regression therapy or hypnotherapy to name but a few. In the US there's a school of therapy called 'sand tray therapy' where participants use trays of sand and small objects to 'create the world of their inner reality' and use the sand tray as a mirror in which they heal their inner life – whatever works for the Americans!

Addiction Treatment

Addiction problems are specialised and need to be treated differently to physical and emotional problems. Again your GP is a good person to start with. He or she will have seen lots of people suffering from drug addiction, alcoholism, gambling addiction and other addiction problems. Remember, if your ex is suffering from an addiction you may need help and support from one of the specialised organisations for families of addicts. Your local HSE office will give you information on addiction services.

If you have a drug addiction problem and you live in Dublin your GP or local heath office may recommend that you attend the Drug Treatment Centre Board (DTCB) on Pearse Street in Dublin. The DTCB has multi-disciplinary teams and experienced doctors and psychiatrists who specialise in giving a primary care service to clients suffering from drug addiction.

Other addiction services are available in the Ana Liffey Drug Project, Council for Addiction Information and Mediation, Coolmine Therapeutic Community and Merchants Quay Project, Dublin; the Aisling Group and Bradan Foundation, Co. Meath; Cuan Mhuire, Co. Kildare; the Hanly Centre, Dun Laoghaire; and the Arbour House Treatment Centre in Cork.

There are private clinics in Ireland and England that offer different methods of helping you overcome your drug addiction. Drug addicts are given help to detoxify in the community or on residential treatment programmes and provided with medication where it is needed.

There are different types of therapies available for alcoholics. Again they will be helped to detoxify and given medication to help with cravings, moods and anxiety in a residential or home setting via their local health service or from a GP.

Alcoholics Anonymous (AA) has a twelve-step programme that is used worldwide to help people recover from alcoholism. It doesn't provide detoxification or residential treatment. It's voluntary and confidential and people get together to share their experiences and find information on how to cope. Another organisation called Alcohol Rehab Ireland bases its treatment of alcohol addiction on bio-chemical repair after abstinence is achieved.

Gambling is recognised by the medical profession as a compulsive illness and treatment for gambling addiction is available in Ireland. The Rutland Centre in south Dublin provides treatment for gambling addicts. There is a Gamblers Anonymous organisation in Ireland which provides help and support to members who wish to solve their gambling problem. They organise meetings in different locations in Ireland.

Al-Anon and Gam-Anon provide help to and support for friends and families of people who are suffering from alcohol and gambling addictions.

If you have health insurance you may be covered for private residential treatment for your addiction. A fuller list of helpful organisations and their contact details are given in the resources section at the end of this book.

Advice from Family and Friends

Irish people love getting involved, knowing all the details of your life and giving advice – and that's just your acquaintances! The best kind of help that family and friends can give you if you're going through a lot of grief after a break-up is active listening and practical support.

A friend or family member who will listen to you is a true friend. Being allowed to talk through what has happened without contradiction, interruption or advice is the best thing for you at the initial stages. Later, when you've got over the shock, it's helpful to hear other people's stories and their advice, but in the beginning you will need people around you who can offer a sympathetic ear.

Friends and family who offer practical support are invaluable. If they are willing to pay special attention to your children and help with cooking, shopping, childcare and cleaning they are saints.

Don't allow people who irritate you or load you with unasked for or unwelcome advice to get on top of you. During this difficult time the people who are truly kind and wise will be apparent. Loyal, positive friends who are willing to give and be honest with you are worth their weight in gold.

An advantage of being down at this time is that your true friends will become apparent. Don't allow toxic friends or 'frenemies' (enemies disguised as friends) space in your life. If your friend or family member makes you feel worse after you've spent time with them then don't spend time with them.

Learning Conflict Resolution Skills

Conflict theory and conflict resolution are fascinating subjects, and if you study them they will provide you with skills for dealing with break-ups and conflict that arises in your life in general. Many academics spend years studying the subject or teaching the skills to others.

Some lucky people are instinctive peacemakers – they can go into a tricky or dangerous situation and by using their charm, intelligence, perception or strength of personality resolve the conflict. Everyone else can learn conflict resolution skills from books or courses. People who study conflict resolution often work as mediators – neutral third parties who help warring couples, communities, parties or countries resolve disputes.

Here is some basic information that will introduce you to thinking about conflict resolution and ways of acquiring conflict resolution skills:

- Think of conflict as an opportunity: conflict theorists suggest that conflict should be seen as a signal, a positive rather than a negative phenomenon, and that dealt with properly it can lead to the improvement or transformation of relationships.

- Put yourself in the other person's shoes and try to understand things from their position. If you have enough imagination and you can put yourself in your ex's position then you will be better able to understand where they are coming from.

- Often when emotions are high the people who are involved in a conflict with each other have stopped communicating, demonised each other or reached a mutually hurting stalemate. Strange as it may seem, this can be the point when things can be healed and settled because everyone is totally fed up and afraid. Sometimes it takes the intervention of a trusted third party to bring about the change.

- What are conflict resolution skills? People who practise conflict resolution as mediators or international peacekeepers use some of the following techniques. Remember that not all situations can be resolved by using mediation or conflict resolution skills and that often it only works because of the skill, experience and personality of the conflict resolution expert.

  ○ Reflective or active listening – it helps when you are listening to someone to repeat the gist of what you have heard to show that you understand what is being said to you.

  ○ Studying personality types – understand and think about the type of person you are dealing with. An aggressive, defensive personality type will need different handling to a timid, frightened person in a high-conflict situation.

○ Reframing problems – it helps to reframe a problem in a way that is non-toxic. For example, if someone says to you that the problem is 'You are so mean you're making me and the children starve to death' you might reframe it by saying, 'I think the issue we're dealing with here is your lack of financial resources.'

○ Uncovering interests behind positions – people in conflict have interests that they hide. They may take a position that seems rigid but if you can uncover what your ex really wants as opposed to what they say they want you may be able to satisfy that interest. For example, your ex may say that they will never leave the family home but that is not really their true interest; it is their position. Their interest may be in living in a particular area.

○ Remain calm and impartial – remember that your aim is to resolve the conflict. The best mediators are always people who keep calm in situations of high conflict. Bertie Ahern remained extraordinarily calm while negotiating the Northern Ireland peace process, for example.

○ Check body language – be aware of whether your body language is aggressive or threatening. Witnessing someone shaking their fist, pacing furiously or hitting inanimate objects can be terrifying. Sitting down calmly face to face and keeping still can go a long way to reassuring a person who is intimidated. Symbolic gestures at crucial times can mean a lot in the context of a high conflict situation. Think of the memorable handshakes in the context of the Northern Ireland peace process. You don't always have to talk to your co-parent but making good eye contact or giving a wave goodbye to a co-parent after dropping children off can be reassuring and help to diffuse conflict.

○ Remember that conflict resolution is a skill that mediators and other professionals spend years studying and role-playing so they can practise them to help others. Don't expect to be able to resolve conflict in your own life by reading these paragraphs. If you are interested and serious about gaining conflict resolution skills you can study it by reading books or doing courses. There is a list of suggested reading on mediation and conflict resolution at the end of the book.

Making a List

Lists are a great way of clearing your mind and setting an agenda for what needs to be done. If you are worried about all the things you have to do then writing them down as a list can give you clarity and a plan. Be realistic when you make a list. Divide it into things that need to be done immediately and things that need to be done in the longer term. You're sure to be distracted and upset following a break-up and it's a bad time to become disorganised and forgetful.

If you have time in the morning or the evening make a list of the things you need or want to do. If you have an app on your phone or a little notebook that you keep with you, you can add to your list during the day. Making a list will help you stop worrying about things when you're trying to sleep. When you write you use different senses – you are writing, seeing and thinking about your goals for the day and they impress themselves on your mind in a much stronger way than they would if you just thought about them. As you complete each task tick it off and this will boost your self-confidence as you go through the day.

Below is a suggested list of things you can consider putting on your agenda:

Personal:
- Make an appointment to see your GP for a full medical
- Make an appointment to see a counsellor or therapist
- Book a de-stressing massage
- Go for a walk, for example Dalkey Hill, the Burren walk, the Glen of Aherlow
- Attend an exercise class
- Join a gym

Family and friends:
- Telephone sibling or friend for chat
- Accept invitation to stay with parents/family
- Have friend(s) around for DVD and pizza
- Meet friend/family member for coffee/lunch

Long-term goals – improving your career:
- Make an appointment with an employment agency
- Investigate further education or a night course
- Write an article for a journal

Don't rush the process of getting over the shock of your break-up and expect to feel good quickly. Take your time and try some of the things suggested in this chapter. Hopefully at least one of the things you have read here will help you on your journey to getting over the initial pain and trauma of your break-up.

2

Putting Children First

*Being a good parent – Your child's rights – Your child's financial
security and maintenance – Guardianship, custody and access –
Making a parenting plan – Your child's emotional well-being*

Being a Good Parent

Parenting after a break-up or on your own is a huge challenge. The traditional family unit of mother, father and children aren't going to be located under one roof and you will need to communicate, negotiate or litigate with your co-parent so that you can creatively and sensitively organise your joint parenting.

If you want to be good parents then you must both set a good example to your children and put their needs ahead of your own. If your co-parent decides that he or she is going to behave badly that does not mean that you have to do the same. If your ex behaves in an appalling manner towards you or in front of your children the desire for revenge can cloud your judgement. Nothing can be solved definitively without a court order or the consent of you and your ex. Sometimes court orders will be ineffective if one person refuses to cooperate. If your ex is damaging your children by his or her behaviour you may reach a point where you must refer your problem to lawyers, social workers or mental health professionals.

Parents who decide to take responsibility for their children should do so wholeheartedly and with love. Children depend on adults for everything and should be accorded dignity, respect and the best care you can give them. Going through a break-up is not a reason to absolve yourself of that responsibility.

If you don't have children to mind and you're going through a distressing break-up then your main responsibility is to look after yourself so you can work and interact healthily with friends and family. However, if you do have children then you have a greater responsibility. Your duty is to keep yourself as healthy, sane and informed as possible so that you can parent well and protect your children as best you can from any difficulties and conflict that may arise after a break-up.

Think back to the time when you were a teenager. You were able to spend hours mooning and dreaming about your girlfriend or boyfriend. If you don't have children now then you can probably still make long phone calls to your friends, indulge yourself a little and as long as you can drag yourself into work or continue your education then the rest of your life is your own.

If your income hasn't dropped dramatically and your friends haven't forgotten you life can roll on and hopefully your broken heart will mend. If you're really lucky you may even be able to go home to your parents for a weekend of TLC.

Life is very different when you break up with a co-parent and you have children to look after. You can't afford to have a long meltdown, either emotionally or physically. Babies need to be fed and children have to be brought to school. As a parent you can't shut down and hide under your duvet, no matter how much you feel like it.

Breaking up with a co-parent is much harder than breaking up with someone with whom you have no children because your lives are intertwined and you have joint responsibilities towards your children. If you want to be good parents you will try to prevent the damage and disturbance of your break-up from having a detrimental effect on your children. The combination of dealing with your own personal hurt and the hurt of your children can be overwhelming.

If your break-up is overwhelming and you feel you can't cope then you should try to get help. Ask your friends and family to take your children for an afternoon if you're having a meltdown or suffering from exhaustion. Most parents are wisely reluctant to expose their children to their emotional turmoil, and if you genuinely aren't functioning then it's better to remove yourself from your children for a few hours and seek professional help from a counsellor or doctor.

Working Together with Your Co-Parent

Suddenly being away from your children because you've left the family home, or being left on your own with them full-time, requires adjustment for both co-parents and children. As parents you both need to cooperate as much as you can to make this very difficult adjustment as painless as possible for your children. To do otherwise is selfish, immature and egotistical.

Working together as co-parents post break-up is not easy for either parent if they are both genuinely putting children first. If you have left your children to live away from the family home you will need to work hard to provide an alternative space and time where you can parent away from the family home. This can be hugely problematic for co-parents (often fathers) who don't have the resources to create a space where their children can hang out and spend the night, or lack the finances for treats and special days out.

If you are the parent who is living with the children in the family home you will probably have to adjust to less income and the withdrawal of support with household responsibilities and childminding from your ex. You may find you have a lot more to do with less help available to you.

Both parents will need more energy and have to make an extra effort if they don't want their children to suffer.

If your aim post break-up is to make things as difficult as possible for your co-parent you will also be hurting your children. The more difficulties you put in the way of your ex the more you may affect his or her ability to parent or maintain a healthy relationship with your children. By doing this you are hurting your children. If you want to play a positive role as a parent in your children's lives you should not do this.

To be a good parent in a break-up is a huge challenge. You may not always succeed. Sometimes the urge to say horrible things about your ex or fight in front of your children is impossible to resist. If your ex is making life difficult for you by not turning up to see your children, trying to use your children against you, failing to pay maintenance or generally torturing you you must deal with those issues in the proper way. Involving children in adult issues is unfair, damaging and inadvisable.

Many children in Ireland live primarily with one parent; that may be because that parent is widowed, but usually it's because their parents are separated, divorced or not present in their lives. Many other children live in families where there is another adult present in the house who is not their parent but is a step-parent, foster parent, grandparent or partner of their parent.

Statistically, children are at a disadvantage when their parents live apart from each other. They are more like to live in poverty and suffer from social, psychological and emotional problems; but that is not to say that many, many children parented by lone parents don't do well.

There is an argument that couples are better off staying together unhappily rather than separating as it can be better for the children. However, if your children are in a dangerous or detrimental atmosphere or they are being subjected to physical or emotional violence then you should seek advice and help around those issues. The decision to end a relationship is a difficult one but the welfare of your children must be the overriding factor. There is no doubt that many couples do stay together in unfulfilling relationships because they don't want to break up the family unit. It's up to individuals and couples to make that decision for themselves. Children can have problems when they come from completely harmonious families, and some wonderfully balanced people grow up in highly dysfunctional family situations.

If you are separated, divorced or living apart from your co-parent it is up to you and your co-parent to decide how you are going to handle every aspect of your parenting. Each parent's situation is unique. There is a huge range of levels of input or contact that parents can have in relation to the upbringing of their children. Some are better at spending small intense periods of time with their children. Others prefer to be with their children for as much time as they possibly can.

Parenting Alone

If you or your co-parent do not want to have any involvement with your children, and cannot be persuaded to do so, then the other parent must accept that. You cannot force a co-parent to spend time with his or her children if he or she does not want to do so. It is heartbreaking for you and your children to be rejected and it can do long-term damage to children if one parent ceases to have contact with them. If your child is finding the lack of contact with a parent difficult then it is important to seek help and advice from suitably qualified professionals. Your first point of contact should be your GP. For some children it is a relief when they are no longer living with or seeing an abusive parent but for others not seeing a parent can be traumatic and they may need to talk to a therapist who specialises in child psychology or family therapy about the issue.

As a parent it will distress you hugely to know that your co-parent doesn't want to see your children but you must come to terms with it if it is to be the status quo. To constantly rail against the rejection and discuss it interminably will not help your children. It ought to be explained to them in an age appropriate manner. (A therapist or child psychologist will advise you on the best way to approach this.) After that it is not your business to constantly refer to it in a highly emotional manner and make it an ongoing issue in their lives.

Your children may wish to discuss their co-parent's lack of contact with you and you ought to calmly explain the situation in an age appropriate manner. After that let it go. You can mourn the loss of your ex in your own way and you ought to let your children mourn the loss of their parent in their own way.

At some stage in the future a co-parent may decide to become involved in their children's lives again. If this happens then you ought to seek help and advice on this issue. If your child is very young and you think that contact with a co-parent who constantly disappears or is abusive is detrimental to your child then you must think carefully about how to handle the situation. It's heartbreaking to expose a child to a parent who drops in and out of their life or abuses your child emotionally without understanding the effect this is having on their child.

You may decide on behalf of a young child that the irregular contact is upsetting but you will have to apply to court and probably get a psychologist's report or other strong supporting evidence before you can ask a judge to permanently exclude a co-parent from your child's life.

If your child is older you will not be able to make a decision on behalf of your child as to whether they are to have contact with your co-parent. It is not your decision to make. If they want to see a co-parent who has been absent from their lives for a long time it is their right to make that decision.

If you are the parent who has made a decision to be the only constant presence in your child's life you have a duty to maintain and care for your child. The absence of one parent does not mean that your children should suffer a lower standard of care than those in a two-parent family. If you fail in your duty or are abusive towards your child then you can be subject to supervision and criminal proceedings and, ultimately, the courts can remove your child from you.

Your Child's Rights

Children (who are under the age of eighteen) are vulnerable because their voices are difficult to hear and they do not have the same decision-making powers, forums and ability to express themselves as adults do. If children are being emotionally or physically abused, neglected or suffering from poverty they need the state, judges, teachers, healthcare professionals, parents, family, friends and acquaintances to help them. If a child is being abused the abuse must be reported in a way that the law requires. There is more information on child abuse and reporting in Chapter 6.

Children's rights are human rights and children need everything that adults need. They need housing, healthy food, education, healthcare and to grow up in a safe, loving environment. They also need to have their views and opinions taken into account in matters affecting their lives. In Ireland a large number of children suffer from poverty, poor living conditions lacking basic services, a low standard of education, obesity and a low standard of healthcare. Children living in care are at a higher risk of going missing or dying from suicide and drug overdoses.

Children's rights are often defined by what they can't do rather than what should be done for them. For example, children can't work full-time, have a firearms certificate or travel abroad unaccompanied until they are sixteen. The age of sexual consent is seventeen. They can't vote, make a will, sit on a jury, donate blood, get married without special consent, buy a lotto ticket or buy alcohol until they are eighteen.

The Health Service Executive in Ireland has a statutory duty to promote the welfare of children under the age of eighteen who are not receiving adequate protection. The function of the HSE is to identify children who are not receiving adequate care and protection and coordinate information from all relevant sources relating to children in its area. It must have regard for the rights of parents but the welfare of children is paramount and it should give due consideration to the wishes of children. The HSE should also provide childcare and family support services. If a child requires care or protection the HSE has a duty to take the child into care.

Ireland ratified the United Nations Convention on the Rights of the Child (UNCRC) in 1992. This means that the Irish state is committed to promoting, protecting and fulfilling the rights of children in Ireland. The Convention states that the family unit should be given protection and assistance, that children need special safeguards because of their vulnerability and that they should grow up in an atmosphere of happiness, love and understanding.

According to the Convention, all actions taken by welfare institutions (in Ireland this is the Health Service Executive), the courts of law and other organisations concerned with children should have the best interests of children as their primary consideration. Article 12 of the Convention is interesting in that it encourages adults to listen to the opinions of children and involve them in decision making in a manner appropriate to their age and maturity. The UNCRC encourages social workers, child-care workers and all other adults responsible for children to use children's opinions when making decisions that affect them. The Convention also says that both parents share responsibility for bringing up their children and should always consider what is best for the child and that governments should help parents by providing services to support them, especially if both parents work.

Children can't take their parents to court and force them to maintain them and children can't decide on their own custody and access arrangements, but they can have input into decisions by giving evidence to a judge or speaking to healthcare professionals and making their feelings known.

There are certain situations during family law proceedings when a judge will appoint a 'guardian *ad litem*' (usually a lawyer) to represent a child's interests if he or she thinks it's necessary. A guardian *ad litem* is normally a person who has expertise in working with children and will give the child a voice in court proceedings. He or she will advise the courts on the child's best interests and the child's wishes in relation to the issues before the court.

A child may also give evidence in relation to his or her wishes with regard to his or her custody and access but judges are understandably reluctant to expose very young children to situations that are daunting or uncomfortable for them. Sometimes parents organise reports from teachers, doctors or therapists to use in court proceedings or a court can order psychiatrists' reports, psychologists' reports or social workers' reports around issues involving children. Judges can then consider these reports with other evidence when making decisions concerning the welfare of children.

The Children's Rights Alliance in Ireland is a coalition of 90 different organisations that are working to further the rights of children in Ireland. The Alliance is campaigning for the full implementation of the Convention and it wants a constitutional referendum to take place to strengthen and reflect the importance of children's rights and to ensure that their best interests are always put first.

The Children's Rights Alliance feels there is a need for a referendum because the rights of the family are stronger than the rights of the child in Ireland and this can work against children in some circumstances.

The Ombudsman for Children in Ireland is an office that was set up in 2002. Its functions are to promote the rights and welfare of children and to investigate complaints made by children or on behalf of children against public bodies, schools and hospitals. Contact details for the Ombudsman for Children in Ireland are in the resources section at the back of this book.

Your Child's Financial Security and Maintenance

Everyone has a choice as to how they organise their own finances, but when you have a child you have a different level of responsibility. Living in poverty as an adult is appalling. Homelessness and financial pressure can lead to serious mental and physical health problems or suicide; when you have children relying on you as well then your problems are even greater. If you only have yourself to worry about you might be able to borrow some money, apply for social welfare or make do. If you haven't got a job you might be able to move abroad or seek help from friends and family in the short term. Children can't make decisions about their finances – they rely on adults to look after those issues for them and if the adults they rely on have no options that is a huge problem for children.

As soon as people become parents they need to think in the longer term about financial planning for themselves and their children. Children need stability and security. Your financial status and that of your child are inextricably linked and you ought to take particular care of your own financial well-being (see Chapter 5) in order to provide as well as you can for your child.

Maintainence for Children

Parents in Ireland, whether they are married or unmarried, have a legal responsibility to maintain their children. Maintenance for children is usually made by a weekly or monthly payment or it can be made by a lump sum payment. It is more convenient for both parents if the money is paid on a specified date into a bank account by direct debit. Some co-parents have informal maintenance agreements or no agreements and maintenance is paid sporadically or not at all. Unless you decide to take your co-parent to court he or she will not have to pay maintenance. If you have applied for the One-Parent Family Payment from the Department of Social Protection you will be required to make an effort to obtain maintenance by mediation or by making an application to court.

Generally, when co-parents live apart one co-parent will have primary custody of the children and the other parent will pay maintenance and have regular access arrangements to spend time with their children. (Custody and access are discussed in a separate section below.) Some parents have joint custody arrangements and the children spend equal amounts of time with both parents. Usually the mother has custody and the father pays maintenance and has access arrangements, but there are many fathers who have custody of their children and mothers who have access arrangements and pay maintenance. Technically, a situation could arise where a wealthy custodial mother could be ordered to pay maintenance for the children to a non-earning father who has regular access, but this would not be the norm.

The law treats the issue of maintenance separately to the issues of custody and access so if you're paying maintenance for your children you do not have an automatic right to custody or access to your children.

Maintenance may be paid voluntarily by an informal agreement or by a formal agreement negotiated by both parents themselves with or without legal advice or by using alternative dispute resolution (ADR). See Chapters 3 and 4 on ADR and litigation. If you can't agree on maintenance then either parent may apply to court and ask a judge to decide on the issue. Many cases are settled at the door of the court in these circumstances. You ought to get legal advice on an offer of maintenance if you are unsure if it is fair. If you have agreed on a figure and method for the payment of maintenance you may decide to ask the judge to make the details of the amount and method of payment a court order so that the parent who is applying can go back to court and seek a remedy for non-payment of maintenance if your co-parent defaults in the future.

A judge can award maintenance to a child who is under the age of 18 or up to the age of 23 if the child is in full-time education. If your child is physically or mentally disabled and cannot support him or herself then there is no age limit for maintenance.

If you apply for maintenance in the District Court the limit of the maintenance award is €150 per week and a maximum lump sum payment of €6,348.69. The possible amount of maintenance awarded in the Circuit Court is unlimited.

The amount of maintenance a judge will award will depend on the needs of the child and the financial circumstances of the parents. A judge will be well aware that different children require different amounts of maintenance depending on their circumstances. There is a huge spectrum of possible standards of living between the incomes of different families and judges are aware of this and will take into account the income of both parents and the needs of the children.

The co-parent applying for maintenance ought to bring in evidence of his or her income, assets, savings and expenditure, especially expenditure in relation to their children. The co-parent who is being brought to court for maintenance ought to bring in evidence of his or her income, assets, savings and expenditure to maintain him or herself and all expenditure that he or she spends that is to the benefit of the children.

If you agree maintenance or a judge makes an order for your co-parent to pay maintenance to you, the agreement or order will usually specify the amount of maintenance, a date of payment (day of the week or month) and a method of payment (usually into a bank account or into the court). Sometimes maintenance payments are linked to the consumer price index so that they increase each year in line with inflation.

The Non-Payment of Maintenance

How you organise maintenance for your children as separated co-parents is unique to your particular situation. If there is high conflict between you and your co-parent, or you are both under financial pressure, he or she may be unwilling to pay maintenance for your children. If your co-parent is failing to contribute financially towards the upkeep of your children there is a temptation for many parents to keep their children from having access to the defaulting parent. This achieves nothing and it may very well prolong the conflict and hurt your children.

It is difficult but the best thing to do is to allow your children access to the maintenance-defaulting co-parent and take the issue to the forum where it belongs – the courtroom. Go to court and make an application for maintenance if your co-parent refuses to adhere to a voluntary agreement; bring the agreement into court with you and show it to a judge. If you have an oral agreement for maintenance payment and evidence of past payments bring that evidence into court. If there is already an order in place go back to court and ask the judge to sanction your co-parent for his or her failure to pay maintenance. If keeping your child from having access to your co-parent does force him or her to pay maintenance you will have to judge for yourself if it was worth it. Have you irrevocably damaged relations between you, your child and your co-parent?

If you can't pay maintenance because your financial circumstances have changed you will have to bring in evidence of the change in your circumstances and apply to court to have the maintenance order varied.

If your co-parent fails, neglects or refuses to pay maintenance on a regular basis then keep a record of the times it isn't paid and go back into court and tell the judge what is happening. There's no point tolerating non-payment of maintenance and complaining about it. If you go back into court the judge will use his or her powers to sanction your co-parent until he or she pays up.

If your co-parent fails to comply with a court order for maintenance then the court can order that his or her employer deducts the maintenance from his or her earnings or that the maintenance be deducted from his or her pension. If a defaulting co-parent is self-employed then you can apply for an enforcement order. Judges have the power to regard a failure to pay maintenance as a failure to comply with an order of the court. This is regarded as contempt of court and judges have the power to deal with contempt by imprisonment of the defaulter.

It's important to keep financial matters separate from other aspects of your joint parenting. Young children need to be protected from conflict between adults in relation to these issues. If your ex won't pay maintenance you must deal with that matter through dispute resolution forums and the ultimate sanctions imposed by a judge. As children mature and become older financial issues will become apparent to them, but when they are very young it is information they don't need to know about.

If your co-parent is living abroad and defaulting on his or her maintenance payments an Irish maintenance order can be enforced in all countries that are parties to the UN Convention on the Recovery Abroad of Maintenance Payments.

Managing Your Finances

If you're bringing up your children apart from your co-parent then you are probably under physical, financial and emotional pressure. Children can be incredibly expensive to support. Most parents want to spend whatever money they have on getting the best of everything possible for their child: healthcare, food, household expenses, clothing, computer games, parties, treats, sports gear, toys, books, grinds, family holidays and school trips – it can become a bottomless pit of spending if you let it.

Your child will probably want what his or her peers have. If you lived in a rural African village the chances are your child wouldn't want the latest computer games because their friends wouldn't have them. If you grow up in Ireland there are certain things that nearly every child will want. Television, advertising and marketing force children to become consumers from a very early age.

It takes a really strong-minded parent and an unusual child to be able to resist the pervasive influence of an advertising- and marketing-generated desire for the latest toy or computer game. It's very difficult, but it is good to learn how to say 'no' to your child. It has to be explained firmly and lovingly from an early age that money is not available for certain things.

If your child needs grinds for his or her exams or all the children in your child's school are going on a school trip then your child will want or need those things too. It's hard to make these decisions when you have to be realistic about your financial circumstances. School trips, grinds, holidays and clothing for your child are all very expensive, and if paying for them is going to leave you unable to pay your mortgage or feed your family then you will have to think twice about your priorities.

If you are worried about the standard of education in your local schools do some research and try to find one that is the best fit for your child. Nowadays there are traditional Catholic schools, new multi-denominational schools run by Educate Together and Gaelscoileanna that all produce good Leaving Certificate results and happy children.

Your input as a parent is vital to your child's success in later life. If you take an interest in your child's education and encourage them to study, play sport and participate in beneficial extracurricular activities you are almost certain to increase their mental well-being and career prospects in later life. It's not all down to the school. League tables are deceptive because the schools that do very well on those tables usually have children who are already advantaged from an educational and socioeconomic perspective; in other words, they'd probably do well anyway.

Your access to funds for the maintenance of your children will be limited to what you and your co-parent can afford. Sometimes grandparents, friends and other family members will chip in and pay for treats or give presents. These are obviously very welcome, but occasionally these presents can take decision making out of the hands of the parents or affect your parenting decisions. If a family member takes your child out on a fun trip or activity that you cannot afford it can make you feel hurt or jealous. But children value your company above everything so make sure you participate in activities with your children; they don't always have to be expensive.

Be clear with friends and relatives about what is acceptable and unacceptable – a present of the latest expensive games console from an uncle or aunt may mean that your child spends too much time playing games and that you will have to fund the expensive games your child wants to play on it.

Budgeting is very important when it comes to children. (See Chapter 5 on finances.) Write a list of all the things that you and your children *need* and separate them from the things you and your children *want*. Children's needs are basic. They are the things all humans need – food, clothing, shelter and love. After that everything else is what you want for your children. Make sure you prioritise wisely. There may be a good second-hand shop nearby that sells decent clothing, a state-funded school that has fantastic teachers or sports activities that are free. You don't need a house with a garden if you live near a park. You don't need a car if you live near your child's school and activities and have decent public transport options.

Bad decision making can lead you to create a big expensive headache for yourself. If you decide that your child has to go to a certain school, you have to live in a certain area or you have to have a huge garden because you perceive these things as being vital to your child's well-being then you may condemn yourself to misery. You could end up spending hours in a car that costs a fortune, listening to moaning from your children because everyone in their class has stuff they don't have, and exhausting weekends spent driving them all over the place for sports activities and parties you can't afford and they don't enjoy.

Guardianship, Custody and Access

Guardianship

Married parents and mothers are automatically guardians of their children (even if they themselves under 18); unmarried fathers, civil partners and cohabitants are not. An unmarried father can become a guardian if the mother agrees and they sign a joint declaration or if he marries the mother of his child. If the mother does not agree then the unmarried father will have to apply to court for the status of guardian.

If an unmarried father has his name on the child's birth certificate this does not grant him any right of guardianship or give him any parental rights or responsibilities. His name on the birth certificate establishes his paternity subject to a DNA test. If the identity of an unmarried father is in doubt a DNA test can be used to confirm this. There is a presumption in law that a child born within a marriage is the child of the husband.

You cannot use legal means to force a father to become a guardian, or to force a co-parent to live with his or her child or to take his or her child to stay with him or her on holidays or for weekends. You can only use the legal system to oblige the co-parent of your child to pay maintenance. If your co-parent refuses to pay then you must pursue him or her through the courts. Fortunately many co-parents do want to be involved in parenting their child and are willing to support their child financially.

If a relationship ends before a child is born then a pregnant woman may find it difficult to accept that her child's father would have any input into parenting their future child. The courts will allow a biological father to apply for guardianship and it won't base its decision on the strength of the relationship between the co-parents.

It will make its decision based on what's best for the child.

What does guardianship mean? If the mother agrees or the court appoints a co-parent as a guardian (this is always the father as the mother is automatically a legal guardian) this means that he is recognised legally as the child's father. He has a legal duty to properly maintain and care for the child and a right to make decisions about his child's education, healthcare and general welfare.

Fathers who apply for guardianship succeed most of the time and the court bases its decision on whether or not to grant guardianship on what is in the best interests of the child, not what the mother wants. If a father is appointed as a guardian it doesn't mean the child will suddenly start spending half the week living with someone they've never met before. However it does mean the child's father will have the right to apply to the court for custody or access.

Children benefit hugely from knowing two parents. Mother and father figures are incredibly important for girls and boys. Children who have positive and active mother and father figures suffer from fewer psychological and behavioural problems, have higher academic achievements and better health, and are less likely to engage in criminal behaviour.

Many women wrongly fear that guardianship will give the father of their child power over them or allow him to interfere in how she parents her child. This really isn't the case in practice. In fact, guardianship gives a low level of rights to men in relation to their children. In Ireland the situation is far from equal. An unmarried father who sincerely wants to be involved in his child's life will find it very difficult to do so if the mother of his child is uncooperative.

Unmarried fathers are in a difficult situation if the mother of their child refuses point blank to let them become involved. For many men the obstacles put in their way can lead them to become obsessed, frustrated and depressed. For many separated fathers it's hard to get involved with a new baby while the mother is breastfeeding and giving very particular care to a newborn. If the new father has a bad relationship with the mother and the child is unused to being away from his or her mother then access can be incredibly difficult.

Even fathers within marriage can feel excluded during the early years of their children's lives. For a father who is not welcome at the maternity hospital or home of his newborn child the loss can be devastating. It can also affect the father's extended family. The choice to put obstacles in the way of contact and parenting can deeply upset new uncles, aunts, cousins and grandparents.

New mothers who resist involvement by unmarried fathers ought to try hard to put themselves in the shoes of their co-parent and imagine how they would feel if they were separated from their child and only allowed access once a week for a few hours. It can be a big problem if the mother feels that the new father is incapable of caring for their child because he is inexperienced with babies, is too rough with the infant or has a drug or alcohol addiction. In those circumstances a concerned mother should seek help from her local HSE area office and if necessary make an application to court for directions in the matter.

Joint or individual counselling or mediation can help in these difficult situations. Some parents demonise their co-parent and can't allow themselves to see him or her in a parenting role. If a child's parent has become involved in another relationship or has other children then this may add to the difficulty.

Unless your co-parent has insurmountable negative behaviour patterns such as violence, abuse, criminal activity, alcohol or drug abuse, or a dangerously unstable mental illness then he or she ought to be accepted as a co-parent if they genuinely want to be involved.

Some mothers fear that an unmarried father's attempts to become involved in their child's life are made in an effort to interfere in her life or gain control over her. If she resists his attempts to become involved in their child's life then their relationship may continue as a high conflict battle over this one issue.

A mother who graciously allows a willing father access to his child may find that she has nothing to fear and her child has everything to gain. If his motivation is to control her or interfere with her life and she makes parenting time available to him then he may decide that he does not want to be involved with the child if that was his only motivation.

The Irish Law Reform Commission recommends in its *Report on Legal Aspects of Family Relationships* that unmarried fathers should automatically become guardians of their children unless it is not in the interests of the child. (For example in situations where the father had raped the mother or the child is born from an incestuous relationship.) The report also suggests that the terms 'guardianship' and 'custody and access' be replaced by the terms 'parental responsibility' and 'day-to-day care and contact'.

The Commission also provisionally recommends that people other than parents or guardians (grandparents for example) ought to have the right to apply for custody or day-to-day care and contact where the parents are unwilling or unable to look after their children. Details of where to find the reports are in the resources section at the back of this book.

What Are your Custody and Access Arrangements?

Custody and access are two different things. Children will normally live permanently with, and be in the day-to-day care and control of, one parent. This parent has custody of the children and in most cases it is the mother. In other cases co-parents will have joint custody of their children. The children may still be living primarily with one parent and seeing less of the other parent but the parents both have equal custody of the children.

Sometimes parents have a joint custody arrangement and the children spend equal amounts of time with both parents. This is unusual but becoming more common. If custody cannot be agreed or mediated between co-parents then one or other parent will have to apply to court. Generally it's a good idea to keep children together and have a stable custody arrangement, whether it is joint parent or single parent custody. The court decides on custody issues by considering what is in the best interests of the children and will rarely separate children.

When one parent has custody of the children the other parent can make arrangements for access. Access may be overnight or weekend long. It may be for one long period or a number of short periods. It can include holidays or not. The court will deny a parent access to a child if it considers it is not in the child's best interests. It may also order supervised access if it deems it appropriate.

Grandparents have certain rights in relation to their grandchildren. They may apply to the District Court for access if they are being denied access to their grandchildren. If they are the main carer of their grandchildren they may apply to the court for maintenance from the children's parents, may have Child Benefit and other benefits transferred to them and may also apply to the court to become guardians if both parents die or to adopt if appropriate.

Making a Parenting Plan

A parenting plan in one of the most important documents two parents living apart will ever draw up together. If it is done properly it can provide children with security and certainty in their lives and minimise conflict between co-parents.

This section will answer the following questions:

1. What is a parenting plan?
2. Why is a parenting plan a good idea?
3. How do you draw up a parenting plan?
4. What should a parenting plan contain?

What Is a Parenting Plan?

A parenting plan is a document that sets out all the aspects of parenting that two co-parents want to agree to. It can contain anything relating to the parenting of the co-parents' child or children. You can put in arrangements in relation to custody, access, residency, holidays, education, discipline or anything else you choose. Parenting plans aren't something that Irish people are familiar with. Parents who decide to separate in the US and Australia are encouraged to make comprehensive parenting plans by the courts.

In Ireland, if you're getting divorced or going through judicial separation proceedings then you must supply the court with an affidavit of welfare in relation to your children. It's like a mini parenting plan and usually a solicitor will help you draw it up. The document is then sworn by the parent to verify that it is true and accurate. An affidavit of welfare contains the following information: your personal details; your children's personal details – names and dates of birth; the arrangements for your children's accommodation, education and training; childcare details; maintenance payments agreed or made by court order; information in relation to contact with parents, i.e. access; healthcare agreements; and any care or court proceedings. It's a legal document and it isn't as comprehensive as a parenting plan can be.

If you're not married to your co-parent or you separate without going to court you may never even think of drawing up a parenting plan unless you are encouraged to do so by a government agency, mediator, parenting expert or lawyer.

Why Is a Parenting Plan a Good Idea?

Everyone who lives apart from their co-parent should seriously think about drawing up a parenting plan. They may not stick to it but it will provide a helpful framework for your joint parenting. Even the process of drawing up a plan can be beneficial as it gives both parents time and space to discuss aspects of parenting they may not have thought about.

Sitting down together to draw up the plan might have the added advantage of improving your relationship with your co-parent. It can actually change how you both relate to each other. If you can learn to work together and cooperate in relation to your parenting it can have an impact on how you relate to one another if problems present themselves in the future. You will be used to discussing issues and consulting with each other.

The most important thing about parenting plans is that they provide children with security in relation to how their day-to-day lives are planned. It shows children that their parents have thought seriously about every aspect of their parenting arrangements and have made them a priority.

How Do You Draw up a Parenting Plan?

If you can communicate amicably with your co-parent and you think you can sit down together comfortably to discuss parenting then you might decide to use the headings from a book or website as a template for drawing up your own parenting plan. It's a difficult thing to do and only works where both parties are confident and have a good relationship.

There is always the danger of power imbalances where two people try to come to agreement without professional advice; very few parents are able to do this. It's always a good idea to ask an independent and neutral third party to look over your plan in case you have missed out on something important.

If you think there is too much conflict between you and your co-parent then you can hire a professional mediator, lawyer or psychologist who is trained in this area. You will probably need a few sessions to draw up the plan.

If the conflict between you and your co-parent is very high and you are communicating through a lawyer you can still draw up a parenting plan on your own and send it to your co-parent for his or her amendments. However, your co-parent may ignore your requests to deal with parenting issues or refuse to meet with the mediator or counsellor. If important issues arise that cannot be dealt with cooperatively then your only recourse is to try to use an intermediary or to seek directions from the court.

Parenting plans are usually drawn up by parents but children ought to be consulted and allowed to have an input where it is possible and appropriate. It's important that input from children is suitable for their age and honest. For example, a teenager might want to spend certain nights with one parent for social reasons, or have a say in holiday arrangements. Younger children will have less input into a parenting plan and professionals can guide co-parents in relation to this aspect.

What should a Parenting Plan Contain?

A parenting plan can contain anything you want to put into it. It can be a calendar on the wall with days marked out on it or it can be a twenty-page agreement drawn up over numerous sessions with a mediator, parenting expert or child psychologist and signed by both co-parents.

The following are a number of headings (they are not exhaustive) that co-parents can consider, discuss and incorporate into a parenting plan:

An Intention Clause

You can start your parenting plan with a clause that expresses the intention of both co-parents to mutually respect each other, not to denigrate each other in front of their children, to cooperate, to communicate effectively and to support each other in their aim to co-parent positively together.

A Financial Clause

If you have a maintenance order or agreement in relation to the children you can incorporate this into the parenting plan. The plan might add to or adjust the maintenance agreement. For example, a parent who is paying maintenance might also want to contribute in other ways by buying presents and clothes, or giving pocket money, spending money for holidays or treats to the children.

Guardianship

Both parents may have settled guardianship by signing a declaration or going to court. The documents in relation to guardianship can also be incorporated into a parenting plan.

Custody

Custody can be agreed between the co-parents or decided in court. If it has been decided in court the order may be incorporated into the parenting plan. If not the parenting plan can specify the arrangements in relation to custody. You may prefer to call it a 'parental responsibility clause'.

Co-parents may choose to be joint custodians of their children or one parent may retain primary care and control of the children. The children may normally reside with one parent, in which case that parent is the primary custodian. If the children are spending a significant amount of time with both parents it is nice to state that both parents have joint parental responsibility of their children as it ensures both parents feel responsible and included.

Access

It's really important to get this right as access can become a battleground for co-parents long after everything else has been settled and agreed. Arguments over pick up, delivery, timekeeping, holidays and clashing schedules are just some of the problems that can arise.

Try to be as detailed as possible in your schedule so that everyone knows what's happening well in advance. You don't need to be rigid if both co-parents are happy with that, but a schedule is a good idea from the children's point of view.

Parents may have different opinions on how flexible a schedule ought to be. If your co-parent is less flexible than you are and prefers a strict adherence to the schedule and timekeeping then you should try to be organised and punctual. It will lead to ongoing irritation and conflict and be very upsetting for your children if one co-parent is continually late or fails to show up at access times.

It's a good idea to drop off your children to your co-parent when their access period starts. It's easier to let children (if they're old enough) off outside a house and less intrusive than calling to the door to pick them up. You may be interrupting or invading your co-parent's space. Another way of making the drop off and pick up easier is to arrange your child's schedule so your co-parent picks your child up from an activity or after school and drops your child back to school.

Some co-parents don't mind seeing each other on a regular basis but where it is difficult or painful they should try to work out a regime that allows them a level of contact with each other that they are comfortable with. It is in the interests of the children that they are exposed to as little conflict as possible and tactful arrangements can help minimise this.

Both co-parents should sit down with a calendar every six months or so and look at the holidays, weekends and weekly access arrangements. If you have a mediator helping you to work out a schedule then you should go through the calendar with them.

In high conflict break-ups the court will have imposed access arrangements but it's usually a fairly basic order. It might refer only to weekends, Christmas and summer holidays. Some parents will stick to the court order and it can work for them. For many others the court order is a starting point. They may go on to fine-tune it and alter it as they go along. It's important for children to have a regular schedule that they are used to.

Examples of types of schedules:

- Equal time: Co-parents decide to share parenting equally and have a one-week-on, one-week-off schedule that continues all year except for holidays abroad.

- Weekend access: One co-parent has custody and access during the week and the other has access at weekends.

- Midweek access: One co-parent has custody and access during the week and the other co-parent has access for one night midweek and alternate weekends.

- Holiday access: If a co-parent lives abroad the custodial parent has school-term-time custody and access and the other co-parent has access during holidays or when he or she visits Ireland.

- Monthly access: One co-parent has custody and access and the other co-parent has one access weekend per month.

Christmas is sometimes shared by both co-parents seeing the children on Christmas Day. One parent may have a family get-together at lunch time and the other at dinner time. One parent may spend the morning with the children while the other parent spends the afternoon with them. Sometimes parents decide to alternate Christmas each year so that the children spend the whole of Christmas with each parent every second year.

Co-parents who live very near to each other will find access arrangements easier to organise. People who are co-parenting should seriously think about trying to live near their co-parent. Some parents even live on the same street or next door to each other so their access arrangements are easier for their children. Ireland isn't a huge country so even if co-parents don't live in the same city or county children ought to be able to spend decent periods of time with both parents.

Practical and Logistical Issues

Living in two places is disruptive for your children so you will have to work extra hard to make sure that your child isn't left with a dirty school uniform or missing toys and games. Co-parents need to be very organised in relation to their children's possessions. It's not fair to hand over a big pile of your children's stuff in a bag to your co-parent at the end of an access period.

If the custodial parent agrees to do the laundry for the children then at the very least dirty clothes should be returned in a laundry bag, clean clothes ought to be folded and put in a separate bag or case, books, and toys and games that travel with your child should have special backpacks or boxes that are kept in the same place at all times.

Some parents like to buy two of certain things so that they don't have to keep moving them between two houses. If you can afford to do this that's a great idea. At the very least children should keep toothbrushes, toiletries, a set of spare clothes and pyjamas in both houses. Computer games, shoes, school uniforms and sports gear are very expensive so most parents will have to pack and unpack regularly and need to be efficient and organised.

Of course children can and do take responsibility for their own things. They should be able to help out and many of them will willingly pack up games and organise their own clothing. As separated co-parents you must take into account that moving between houses is difficult for children and it is your responsibility to make it as easy as possible for them.

Discipline and Curfews

Co-parents need to sit down and seriously discuss their house rules with each other. Children ought to have age appropriate discipline and curfews spelt out to them. As much as possible, co-parents should be consistent in how they approach discipline issues and house rules. If one parent allows a child to live by totally different rules to the other it will be confusing and disruptive and may lead to problems in the future.

Parents may decide on certain rules that have to be adhered to in both houses, for example:

- Homework will be done immediately after school.
- Computer games will be limited to … hour(s) per day/week.
- Television viewing will be limited to … hour(s) per day/week.
- Bedtime is at … o'clock.
- Curfew is at … o'clock.
- Pocket money is €… per week/month.

Other rules in relation to manners, politeness, safety, etc. can be added to the parenting plan. Parents should decide what sanctions to impose on children who break house rules and agree on those sanctions.

Education

Parents ought to set out their intention in relation to the education of their children. Schools, extracurricular activities and potential or intended future schools can be included in this section.

> *An example of an education clause:*
> Our children [names] currently attend St Mary's National School. It is our intention to send them to St Martin's Senior School. At present their extracurricular activities are swimming, tennis and Gaelic football. We both agree to support our children in their education, help them achieve their educational goals, and ensure that they attend all their extracurricular activities.

Information Sharing

Both parents should agree to share information with each other in relation to their children as fully and expeditiously as possible.

> *An example of an information sharing clause:*
> We, as co-parents agree that if [name of child] has to attend a hospital, doctor or other medical practitioner in an emergency or for any other reason that we will inform the co-parent who is not present as soon as possible.

Dispute Resolution

Co-parents should try to incorporate a dispute resolution mechanism into their parenting plan. If disputes arise in relation to the content of the parenting plan or in relation to proposed changes to the parenting plan then they should have a suggested method of dealing with future disputes. This paragraph might suggest mediation and the name of a mediator.

Other Things a Parenting Plan can Contain

- An agreement to shield children from conflict
- An agreed minimum notice period for changes of plan in access arrangements
- Details in relation to who holds passports and where they are located
- A clause in relation to pets and pet care
- An agreement in relation to religious ceremonies or beliefs
- Details of named guardians in the event of the death of a parent
- An agreement to provide for telephone contact with a co-parent at certain times

Your Child's Emotional Well-Being

Your divorce or separation will have an effect on your children. They will have a lot of things to cope with all at once, such as loss of contact with one parent, moving between two houses and heightened conflict between their parents and extended family.

As parents you are in the best position to help your child. If you can shield your child from conflict and disruption and put in place a strong regular structure post separation then you'll be helping to minimise the effect of the break-up on your child's mental health.

The best people for a child to communicate with when he or she is distressed are his or her parents and family. Children need to know that they can come to you to discuss what is happening. If your behaviour is sending a message to your children that you can't cope and you're not there to help them this will distress them further. That is why it is so important that you take care of yourself and your own mental health post break-up (see Chapter 1).

Children are naturally curious and will want to know what is going on between you and your co-parent. Give them information that is age appropriate and if you are in doubt about what is appropriate talk to a professional therapist. Keep your children informed as to what is going on in relation to the living arrangements of their co-parent and the custody and access arrangements. Make sure they are informed and consulted as much as possible.

Chapter 1 is aimed at helping you to look after yourself. There are details in relation to psychiatrists, psychologists and therapists in that section and the resource section at the end of this book that are also useful for your children if you're worried about their mental health. Irish people have no problem taking their child to the doctor if they think they're physically ill, but many parents don't want to bring their child to mental health professionals because they fear their child will be stigmatised.

There is this understandable reluctance to bring children to psychiatrists and psychologists because parents don't want their children to think they have something wrong with their mental health; they also think that as parents they should be able to help their children themselves. However, the best way to help your child is to ensure they get professional help if necessary.

If parents spot signs that their child is distressed they ought to talk to their GP. Signs of distress include loss of interest in activities, self-harming behaviour, increased anxiety, mood swings, loss of appetite, sleep problems, panic attacks, feeling tired, continual crying, isolation and hallucinations. If the signs are acute parents ought to take their child to a mental health professional immediately.

If your child has an eating disorder or is severely depressed, behaving in a violent manner, abusing substances or obviously suffering mentally and unable to cope then you should bring your child to your GP or local health service, or meet your GP on your own and tell him or her about the problems you are having with your child, and he or she will advise you as to who is the best person for your child to go to. If you're not sure whether your child's behaviour is normal behaviour then you ought to ask your GP for advice.

Schools often have specialists who help with mental health problems. If you and your child have confidence in your school and the counsellors available at the school then this is another option.

Parents are normally included in meetings with mental health professionals when children are young and will go to initial appointments with their child. Mental health professionals will usually take a history from the parents at the first session. Different therapists use different types of therapy depending on the age of the child. If your child has a medical or biological problem then a psychiatrist may prescribe medication. For young children play therapy may be appropriate because they can communicate better through play than through talk therapy.

Therapy will help children to communicate their needs and give them tools to cope with whatever trauma they are experiencing. Unfortunately in Ireland it is difficult to access mental healthcare for children. The Children's Mental Health Coalition in Ireland is a lobbying coalition that aims to improve the mental health services for children in Ireland. In the past many children were treated for mental health problems in adult inpatient units and this is unacceptable. The Health Service Executive provides a child and adolescent mental health service that parents can contact through their local health office.

If there are custody, access or maintenance disputes then sometimes one parent will encourage a child to denigrate the other parent. This can result in a situation called 'parental alienation'. The child will express a hatred or unreasonable attitude towards one parent, making access impossible. It can be a confusing issue because if a child is being abused they may express parental alienation towards an abusive parent as a way of protecting themselves.

Parental alienation is complex and happens for many different reasons. It can occur because the child aligns with one parent and that parent then actively undermines a co-parent by constantly criticising or making negative comments. Parents can also alienate themselves by feeling rejected and acting negatively towards their child. If a parent feels rejected by a co-parent he or she may take that out on his or her child by being cold, negative and critical, or withdrawing from the child.

Parental alienation exists but is not recognised by the scientific community as a mental health problem affecting adults. It is obviously emotionally harmful for children to become alienated from one parent. The dynamic of parental alienation must be understood. Is it because of abuse or is it caused by the aligned parent or is the parent causing him or herself to be alienated? Mental healthcare professionals will advise you and your co-parent on the best course of action where a child has become alienated from a parent.

There are formal support services that are specifically aimed at helping children whose parents are going through a break-up. Having a trusted dedicated individual professional can provide children with stability and security and help them to make sense of what is happening. For other children contact with a group of children who are going through the same thing can give them the understanding, comfort and support they need.

Children and their parents can be reluctant to have contact with counsellors and support groups because of fears of teasing, being seen as different, stigmatisation or being thought of as having a mental disorder. Organisations such as See Change are working to remove this stigmatisation. It is vitally important that children receive the help they need. Early intervention makes a huge difference and without counselling and support mental health problems can grow and become unmanageable, and can lead to mental illness and suicide.

Rainbows is a charity that was established in Ireland in 1998. Its aim is to provide children with support after a painful loss such as death, divorce or separation. It now operates in over 600 locations, which are predominantly in school settings; around 2,000 facilitators work with around 15,000 children. The facilitators organise weekly meetings for different age groups with different themes, such as 'facing fear and worries', 'endings and beginnings' and 'weathering the storms – coping tools'.

Teen Between is another specialised support service for teenagers and young adults whose parents are going through a divorce or separation. It is organised by

Relationships Ireland and provides a free specialised teen-age counselling service for one hour a week. It deals with topics such as 'coping with parents', 'surviving school' and 'different perspectives – you and your parents'.

3

Alternative Dispute Resolution

Introduction – The best conditions for ADR – ADR in Ireland –
Mediation – Collaborative law – Counselling

Introduction

Disagreements and disputes almost inevitably arise post
break-up and it is important to think carefully about
how you intend to deal with them. Your motivation is
extremely important. If your intentions are good and you
want to minimise conflict, protect your children and move
on with your life then you will try to use peaceful rather
than aggressive means to resolve your disputes, unless
you have no alternative.

It is always in your interests to try to use peaceful means
to resolve your disputes, because if you encourage high
conflict levels in your life post break-up you will damage
yourself, your financial stability and your relationships
with your family and friends, as well as hurting your ex.

There are three ways of dealing with your disagreements
and disputes with your ex post break-up: you can ignore
them, go to court or use an alternative dispute resolution
(ADR) process. If you decide to litigate, you will have to
hire a lawyer and you will be plunged into a potentially

expensive adversarial situation that can be traumatic and take a long time.

You may have no choice but to litigate if conflict with your ex is high or your situation can't be resolved in another way. If conflict between you and your ex is low, you can't resolve your issues between yourselves and the conditions are right, you ought to try to use an ADR process to resolve your issues. If you manage to draft a separation agreement with an ADR professional, you may or may not decide to hire a lawyer to look at the draft agreement before you both agree to sign it and adhere to its terms. It is always advisable for both parties to a mediated agreement to get legal advice if they intend to sign an agreement that affects property, financial, inheritance or parenting rights. Unless you are extremely well informed you risk signing an agreement that is unfair to you and your children or entering into an agreement that is potentially unenforceable.

ADR is a private and cooperative process; it takes place outside the courts system and normally both parties to the process will hire a mediator, collaborative lawyer or counsellor to help them to resolve their joint issues.

Allowing post break-up issues to remain unresolved isn't usually a good idea. Leaving children without regular schedules, houses in joint names or unsold, and spending unchecked can cause your lives to spiral out of control and small problems can quickly escalate into large ones.

If your lives aren't properly organised post break-up then your children may develop behavioural difficulties because of disorganisation, insecurity and uncertainty. If assets aren't divided, realised or sold and spending isn't checked then financial disaster can ensue.

On the other hand, many people choose to ignore their post relationship issues and spend years in a kind of limbo

– parenting is never formally worked out, houses are left in joint names and financial matters remain static. Sometimes one person moves out to live elsewhere but continues to have a semi-marriage, friendship or relationship with his or her spouse or partner.

There are no laws or rules saying that you have to formally sort out the end of your relationship in a specifically defined manner and chaotic arrangements or loose ties work well for those who like to have their lives and arrangements undefined. If there is enough money to go around and your joint financial situation is working then you may not need to put things on a formal footing. However, if you are co-parenting you ought to work out your arrangements in an organised manner so that your children are happy and secure.

People have different ways of arranging their lives; if you have the ability to creatively organise things between yourselves and everyone is happy with their living arrangements then there may be no need to litigate or engage in ADR.

If your ex has disappeared or has nothing to offer in terms of financial or parenting support then it will be impossible to litigate or use ADR. There are some dysfunctional people who become so caught up in their anger and bitterness that they will use anything and everything around them to cause as much destruction in your life as they can. They might adopt the strategy of refusing to see their children, winding down the family business, refusing to engage in employment or deliberately wasting assets, making it practically impossible to engage in ADR, negotiate or litigate effectively.

If you are in the process of litigating and your ex is trying to obstruct you, a good judge will adjourn the case or make specific orders to halt the destruction until your manipulative ex takes up employment or gets his or her finances back on track. There are situations that are so extreme and high conflict that your ex may decide that he or she won't ever give you any money, even if this means that he or she ruins his or her own financial resources or faces prison.

If you find yourself in a situation where your ex is prepared to go to prison, lose contact with his or her children, devalue your house, destroy your business or remain unemployed forever it is difficult for your adviser or lawyer to help you.

You can try to contact doctors and use the legal system to get to a certain point or in extreme situations it may be the right thing to apply to have your ex sectioned under the Mental Health Acts or arrested if you think it's absolutely necessary, but often people reach a stage where they will have to walk away. Your lawyer will advise you when you've reached the point where it is futile to take your ex to court or to suggest ADR. At that time it will be up to you to try to rebuild your life and deal with parenting and financial matters on your own with no help or support from your ex.

You are the person who will make a judgement call as to whether it is worth spending time and money on a lawyer, ADR expert or other professionals.

A good lawyer or other professional advisor such as an accountant will help you decide if it is worth pursuing litigation or ADR for your own particular problems.

ADR is a loose term that covers a broad range of dispute resolution processes that you can use to resolve your disputes with your ex. An ADR professional has no power to make orders or to enforce his or her suggestions or decisions. He or she will meet with you both and try to help you negotiate with each other and come to an amicable resolution.

The main types of ADR used in Ireland are mediation, collaborative law, counselling and arbitration. Mediation and counselling are the most commonly used processes for dealing with conflict around parenting and finances after relationship breakdown in Ireland; collaborative law is becoming more widely used; and arbitration is a quasi-judicial method of dispute resolution that isn't used for family law issues at all.

The Best Conditions for ADR

ADR Is Best for your Joint Issues

Your issues that are part of your own emotional and psychological pain can only be dealt with by you with the help of your friends, advisers, therapist or doctor. You may think they were caused by your ex but they don't belong to your ex and shouldn't be brought into any alternative dispute resolution meeting where you are both trying to settle your joint issues.

Meeting with an ADR professional and successfully resolving your issues can help with your pain but if you are depressed, lonely or angry you ought to get help from a doctor or therapist.

If you are annoyed because your ex has a new partner, lonely because you haven't met anyone new or sad because you think your children love their new stepmother or stepfather more than you then you ought to seek help on your own. An ADR professional isn't there to help you with your individual needs. He or she is there to help you resolve your joint disputes. A good ADR expert ought to refer you elsewhere if he or she identifies that you or your ex have individual issues that need attention.

Occasionally some relationships break up and quickly transform into very supportive friendships. This is highly unusual and if it works that's great. If you have an ex who is genuinely willing to help you, listen to your problems and offer reasoned and constructive advice then you are very fortunate. Normally your ex won't be able to help you with your pain, and if he or she is communicating with you it may be out of guilt or pity, and the advice you're getting won't come from a reasoned and constructive place.

In some joint ADR sessions the mediator or counsellor will allow you both to discuss issues that cause you to feel angry, depressed or frustrated in the context of other issues that are shared by you both. Mediators and counsellors usually set up one or two storytelling or 'intake' sessions where you can tell your story or explain the history of your break-up. Those sessions may be used by you or your ex to vent your emotions or recount past hurtful behaviour. If this goes on for too long or takes up too many sessions then you are engaging in joint counselling rather than trying to move forward and resolve your current issues.

It is important that the process is constructive and the issues discussed in ADR sessions are your joint issues surrounding your break-up: financial, parenting, practical and logistical issues. If you genuinely want to use ADR to sort out those issues then you can enlist the help of an ADR expert – a mediator, collaborative lawyer or counsellor.

Both Parties must Be Willing and Able to Engage in the ADR Process

Alternatives to litigation will only work if both parties are willing and able to engage in the process. One person can't use counselling, mediation or collaborative law or attend a negotiation or mediation without his or her ex or their representative being present. If your ex is unwilling to commit to the process it is still worth asking him or her to attend one session so that he or she can discover what ADR is and what it can do for you both.

The Law Reform Commission's *Report on Alternative Dispute Resolution* recommends that all family law litigants attend information sessions explaining what mediation can do for them, but it recognises that you can't force people to mediate or negotiate. The nature of the ADR process is voluntary, so if you can't persuade your ex to use ADR and you still need to resolve your issues you will have to hire a lawyer and take the litigation route.

There must be trust between both parties if they want to engage in ADR. Parties attending ADR sessions like mediation or collaborative law are often asked to voluntarily bring documents relating to their respective financial situations. If you don't trust your ex to bring true and accurate information in relation to the issues you are trying to resolve then you can't use ADR.

Information that is shared during ADR ought to be confidential. Mediation discussions can't be used in subsequent court proceedings and mediators may ask you to sign a mediation agreement that states that you won't use the confidential information shared at mediation sessions in court. However, if court proceedings are issued after mediation and you are both required to disclose financial information then you and your ex will be aware of the information disclosed during mediation and know what to ask to be disclosed in the context of litigation. No one is going to 'forget' what they found out in the mediation sessions. You must provide accurate information in court or you run the risk of getting into serious trouble with a judge. If you lie during mediation or collaborative law sessions there will be no sanction from anyone but the process will fail because of lack of trust.

Be careful that ADR is being used for the right reasons. It may suit your ex to delay the start of the litigation process so that he or she can do things that are to their advantage in the meantime. He or she might deceitfully suggest mediation so that he or she has time to hide assets, initiate litigation in another, more sympathetic forum (another country) or use the time to manipulate third parties or alienate you from your children. Always get legal advice if you are worried and remember that you can always initiate litigation and ask for an adjournment so that you can try ADR in the meantime; if it doesn't work you can then continue with the litigation.

ADR will work well if both parties are in a strong enough position to engage in the process. There is no point in trying to use ADR if you are being bullied, there is a big power imbalance between you and your ex or if your ex is using ADR as a way to manipulate you or the legal process.

If you feel unable to communicate with your ex because he or she bullied you during the course of your relationship then you will find it hard to use ADR. You must have enough confidence to sit in a room with your ex and express your wants and needs. If the dynamics of your relationship with your ex are such that you can't communicate in that way because you feel bullied or intimidated, then you ought to engage a lawyer.

Some mediators will see both parties separately and assist them to negotiate. This works well where there is a medium level of conflict or a low level of power imbalance. If a mediator is assisting parties to negotiate he or she should advise both parties to get separate legal advice from lawyers before and during the meetings.

It is impossible to use ADR if you or your children are threatened with violence, you suspect abuse of your child, your ex is suffering badly from alcoholism or drug addiction, or your ex is lying to you and your ADR professional. In those situations you will nearly always need the power and support of a lawyer and the legal system.

A lawyer will always advise you as to what is in your best interests and will represent you and guide you through the litigation process. If you cannot trust your ex or you feel that you don't have the confidence to use ADR then you ought to go directly to a lawyer.

ADR Can Be Used With and After Litigation

ADR professionals can be hired at any stage post break-up and you can use ADR while you are litigating to deal with some of your issues. For example, if you have brought legal proceedings against your ex to resolve financial and parenting issues you can use ADR to resolve your parenting issues. You and your ex can sit down with a mediator or counsellor and use the sessions to draw up a parenting plan and then litigate to resolve your financial issues. Alternatively, you could use collaborative law to resolve all your financial issues and then go to court to resolve custody and access issues.

There are no rules to stop you using whatever methods you like to resolve your issues and using ADR to sort out parenting, for example, might make it easier for you both to cooperate in relation to other issues as they arise.

Often disagreements arise after divorce or separation and you and your ex might have had enough of the time, trouble and expense of lawyers. Again, you can go to an

ADR professional and use the process to resolve your disputes. If there are court orders and legally binding agreements in place you can't use ADR to overrule them but you can make new agreements post separation and divorce that you both feel are tailored to your situation.

Advantages of Using ADR

ADR gives you both control over your dispute resolution. If the conditions are right and you both agree to use ADR then you can decide who to hire, when to go to the sessions and what issues you want to resolve. You and your ex will dictate the agenda with the help of your ADR professional.

ADR can be less expensive. If you don't qualify for legal services from the Legal Aid Board and you go through the court process then you may be faced with a large bill for fees at the end of your case. It's hard to know how much you're going to spend on legal fees until you see how your case is progressing, what issues need to be dealt with and how complicated your case is. When you use ADR you can use the free family mediation service provided by the Legal Aid Board or if you use a private service you will usually pay an hourly rate (the costs are normally shared by both parties) and you can stop at any time. This gives you and your ex a clear idea of how much it will cost and the time to pay as you go along.

ADR is a private dispute resolution forum so you won't have to go to a court or appear before a judge. Very few people enjoy going to court as it is a stressful experience. Often cases are delayed or adjourned and you can be left hanging around the door of a courtroom in a very public environment negotiating and discussing intimate details of your private life in a corridor.

Even if you can well afford to go to court or you do qualify for legal services from the Legal Aid Board it can take a long time to resolve your case. In the meantime you will be left in a financial or organisational limbo. It's hard to parent effectively if you're not sure what your access and custody arrangements are going to be and it's difficult to move on with your life if your financial situation is uncertain. ADR helps both parties to communicate and can help you resolve issues in the short term until all your issues are eventually settled.

Using ADR means that you can potentially improve your relationship with your ex or stop it from deteriorating further. Long, drawn-out, high-conflict and expensive litigation will rarely improve your relationship. If you are both able to sit down together and agree on your joint future and make decisions consensually you have a better chance of having an amicable relationship with your ex in the longer term.

ADR, if it works properly, can provide a credible, cost-effective, dignified and speedy resolution to all the financial and parenting issues that surround the end of a relationship. For those reasons it is always worth going to at least one ADR session with your ex if you think it might work and he or she is sitting on the fence. If the ADR expert explains to your ex what ADR can achieve for both of you he or she might change his or her mind about ADR and decide to use the process rather than opt for litigation.

ADR in Ireland

In Ireland ADR isn't well developed or regulated. It's not joined up to the legal system so a judge can't refer you to a court-approved ADR professional. Anyone with very little training in ADR can call themselves a mediator, arbitrator, advisor or collaborative lawyer. There are many training courses of varying length and quality and a number of professional bodies that regulate the practice of ADR and seek to ensure that their members are properly trained and accredited.

Accreditation means that the ADR professional is a member of a professional body, has achieved a certain level of training and is bound by a code of ethics. An accrediting body should have complaints and disciplinary procedures and professional supervision. Lawyers will be subject to the regulations of their professions if they are members of the Law Society (solicitors) or the Bar of Ireland (barristers). The website for the Bar of Ireland has a special section where you can look up the names and qualifications of lawyers who practise mediation. The contact details for the Bar of Ireland are in the resources section at the end of this book. Many solicitors have a mediation section in their practice, or if they are sole practitioners they have mediation qualifications which they advertise on their websites.

The Mediators Institute of Ireland (MII) is a professional association for mediators in Ireland. It promotes the use of mediation and has a high standard of training and accreditation and skills assessment for practitioner members. Some family mediators in Ireland are accredited by the MII and those who are will have undergone comprehensive education and training in family mediation. Some of the accredited family mediators come from a legal background and some of them do not, so you should check before you hire a mediator whether they have a legal or counselling background. Different members of the MII have different levels of training and accreditation and this is explained on its website. Many of the mediators who advertise on the MII website also provide mediation services through the Legal Aid Board's free family mediation service. The mediators on the MII website are available to work privately and can be contacted via its website – full details are in the resources section at the end of this book.

There are a huge variety of ADR courses; some of them are weekend courses and others run for two years. It's impossible to know exactly how qualified your counsellor, mediator or collaborative lawyer is in the area of conflict resolution but it is helpful if they are registered with the MII or another professional body such as the Law Society or the Bar of Ireland that has a clear code of ethics. If you are hiring an ADR professional you should always ask them where they trained and how long the course was.

The quality and expertise of ADR professionals will vary enormously and many couples who try ADR post break-up are disappointed. Lawyers are trained to be adversarial and ADR is the opposite of adversarial so lawyers who train briefly in ADR might not have the personality or understanding to help you resolve your disputes amicably. ADR practitioners require great perception and listening skills but they also need to understand the issues from a legal perspective. Counsellors are trained to have listening skills but often don't understand the complexities of post break-up issues from a legal perspective. Ideally, an ADR professional ought to have a legal qualification and some sort of mediation, collaborative law or counselling training.

It's important that your ADR professional respects your privacy, provides a confidential service, disposes of records of your sessions, protects individuals whom he or she suspects of being abused and has competence and integrity. He or she should also be clear about the fees that will be charged and assure you that he or she won't appear as a witness in any subsequent legal proceedings.

In Ireland there's no such thing as mandatory ADR. Courts can't insist that litigants in the family courts be directed to mediation but lawyers are obliged by law to give potential litigants a list of conciliators and mediators and to discuss with their clients the possibility of reconciliation, using a mediator or engaging in negotiation. The courts are obliged by law and will always give litigants in family law cases time to negotiate or mediate if they ask for it.

The main type of ADR used by people in Ireland after a relationship break-up is mediation (sometimes called conciliation). The other types of ADR that are most often used are collaborative law and counselling.

Mediation

What Is Mediation?

Mediation is a broad term for a conflict resolution process that can be used for any type of dispute. The Law Reform Commission recommends in its *Report on Alternative Dispute Resolution* that it should be defined as 'a facilitative and confidential structured process, in which parties attempt by themselves, on a voluntary basis, to reach a mutually acceptable agreement to resolve their dispute with the assistance of an independent third party, called a mediator.' A mediator who is invited to intervene should use his or her knowledge, communication skills, mediation techniques and personality to resolve the conflict.

Mediators act to resolve disputes during wars, between victims of crime and offenders, in commercial disputes, personal injury litigation and many other arenas. If you and your ex decide to mediate you will both agree to do so and then you will hire an expert in family mediation to help you to resolve your issues.

Family mediation is a type of mediation and usually follows a particular format. Your mediator should organise a mediation meeting or series of meetings for you and your ex either together or separately. Each meeting or session should have a purpose and follow a particular format. Everything that is said during a mediation is confidential (unless child abuse is suspected) and your mediator should not exhibit bias or take sides.

During these meetings your mediator will use a variety of mediation techniques to help you resolve the issues that are causing conflict at the end of your relationship. There are lots of different types of mediators and many different styles of mediation. As a process it's closer to counselling and collaborative law than litigation.

Joint mediation meetings are only suitable for situations where you are physically able to sit in the same room as your ex. You can both meet a mediator with your lawyers present but normally people mediate over post separation and parenting issues on their own. In some mediations the mediator will situate the two parties in different rooms and 'shuttle' between them but this type of negotiation isn't normally used in family mediations.

Solicitors who encourage their clients to go to mediation may continue to represent you or give you legal advice. If the mediation fails they can then act for you if you decide to litigate. A solicitor shouldn't act as a mediator for you and your ex if they are your legal advisor initially because he or she is no longer neutral or impartial or will be seen as biased by your ex. If you both decide to use a mediator who is also a solicitor or a barrister then it ought to be a mediator you have chosen together and not someone who has previously given either of you legal advice.

Mediation can save you time and money, if it works. It can also be a more dignified and less painful way of ending your relationship than a long drawn-out court case.

Who Should You Hire as a Mediator?

Lots of people are trained as mediators in Ireland and there are many mediators available to hire but you should check very carefully before you decide who to use as mediation is unregulated in Ireland – anyone can call themselves a mediator. Mediators have usually completed a course or had some mediation training but you should ask what course they did as you may discover that their training was just a weekend course and that they have very little experience.

The Irish Family Mediation Service (FMS) is run by the Legal Aid Board. It provides a free service to couples who are separating. Its mediators come from different professional or training backgrounds before they trained as mediators. The FMS helps couples who are separating or divorcing to negotiate their own agreements in relation to living arrangements, parenting, property, financial matters and any other problems that arise post break-up.

Both parties must contact the service and confirm that they are willing to attend and then an appointment will be set up. The mediation sessions usually last about an hour and at least two to six sessions are organised. The service is also available to unmarried, gay and lesbian couples. The family mediators who practise with the FMS are accredited by the Mediators Institute of Ireland (MII). Some of the MII mediators in private practice also practise in the free Family Mediation Service.

Many solicitors and barristers are also mediators and can be contacted via the Bar Council or the Law Society of Ireland. Friary Law, Mediation Forum Ireland and the Chartered Institute of Arbitrators – Irish Branch also have details of accredited mediators accessible through their websites. Their qualifications and experience will vary enormously. Some of them will have done a weekend course and others have a doctorate. The qualities that make a good lawyer – problem solving, communication, presentation and advocacy – don't necessarily make for a good mediator, so be careful to hire a lawyer who is fully trained and experienced in the art of mediation.

Counsellors or therapists in private practice also offer mediation services. If they have only completed a short course and have very little experience they may not be the best service to use for post break-up issues. If you have complicated issues involving a family business, debts, property, pensions or maintenance your counsellor may not be sufficiently trained or informed as to the matters that need to be addressed or the implications of the negotiations. Counsellors and therapists may have other professional qualifications or be members of professional bodies that have particular ethics or codes of conduct. Chapter 1 gives information on different types of counsellors and therapists that are available and the different organisations that train and regulate them.

If you decide to hire a counsellor who is using the mediation process as a form of therapy rather than assisting you to negotiate your issues be sure that that is what you want from your sessions. Ask your counsellor or therapist what they aim to achieve during the mediation. Is it about resolving emotional issues or deciding on how to divide assets? If for example, you are attending mediation to deal with financial matters rather than parenting then you might prefer to use a mediator with a professional legal qualification rather than a psychologist or psychotherapist.

What Happens During Mediation?

There are no 'rules' about what can and cannot be done during mediation. Many family mediators are trained in the same way and follow a code of conduct so in Ireland most sessions follow the same guidelines.

A mediator will only agree to mediate if both parties contact them. They must both make an appointment and show up and the cost of mediation, if you are not using a free service, is normally shared between the two parties.

In Ireland the Legal Aid Board provides a free mediation service delivered by the Family Mediation Service. Fees for private mediators vary hugely. Counsellors may charge between €50 and €100 per hour, and lawyers and MII members can be more expensive – €200 per hour and upwards. Make sure you know what the fees are going to be before you start.

Mediators are bound by their code of conduct (if they follow one) to act neutrally and impartially. This means that they cannot take sides. If one party is being obviously bullied by the other the mediator must try to 'power balance', which is extremely difficult. For that reason it is important that mediators direct participants towards legal advisors or suggest they get support from a therapist, family member or friend if they suspect that one party is being pushed into an unfair agreement. If participants in the mediation process have a problem with the process it is usually because they perceive that the mediator is biased towards their ex and pushing them to make a decision that is not fair to them.

If a mediator suspects that the participants in a session have a problem with addiction, alcohol, domestic violence, or mental illness then he or she will provide information for referral to the appropriate service. A mediator can mediate when these problems exist if they aren't severe.

It's up to the mediator to make a judgement call. If child abuse is suspected the mediator ought to report his or her suspicions to the appropriate authorities.

Some mediators like to work in pairs. This is called co-mediation. Sometimes one of the mediators is a trainee and the other is more experienced. For family mediations your mediation service may suggest that you use a male and female mediator for your mediation sessions. This is because the mediators believe that a gender balance reduces the perception of bias by the parties to the dispute.

At the first mediation session the mediator will explain what mediation is and what you can hope to achieve, explain the code of ethics he or she follows, establish ground rules, assure you that the mediation is confidential and take down all your details. The mediator usually sets out the ground rules to the sessions. Both parties should respect and listen to each other. The mediator may ask you both to sign an agreement to mediate.

The rest of the session or the next session is usually an intake session so the mediator will be gathering information and encouraging you both to tell him or her why you are there and what you hope to achieve. He or she might ask you both to tell your stories and ask what happened in your past that brought you to the point of being in mediation together.

Some mediators will see both parties individually before the first session. There are no hard and fast rules about how the sessions are structured. Sometimes the mediator will know in advance that you are both there to discuss one thing, for example parenting, and if there isn't too much conflict you will be able to deal with the issue quickly.

The process will take longer when you don't know what you want to discuss and there is a lot of conflict. The mediator will help you both to draw up a list of your issues and tell you if you need to gather information (for example financial records) for the next session.

Mediators aren't supposed to offer legal or financial advice but if your mediator is an experienced lawyer they will spot issues that may need attention from an accountant or another lawyer and they should flag them for your attention.

When you have figured out the issues you want to try to resolve with your mediator and you have all the information you need available the mediator will then help you to develop options. He or she may throw out ideas to get you going. You both will then be encouraged to suggest options to the mediator.

The mediator will work to redefine your positions in a non-toxic manner. He or she will try to name your issues without the negative or emotional content that you and your ex can attach to them, for example 'joint parental responsibility' or 'finances'.

Your mediator will try to help you to figure out what the actual issues are and what the interests and needs of the family are as opposed to the positions that you are both taking. If you or your ex is insistent on a particular position your mediator will help you to discuss your position and the reason behind it in order to discover if the position is in your family's genuine interest. If positions are not the same as interests the mediator will try to help you to redefine these positions. Once your positions have been redefined by the mediator you will be guided through a bargaining process.

If the process works the mediator will help you both to draft up a document that looks like a separation agreement. In order to give that document legal effect you ought to both take it to your separate lawyers before you sign it.

Sometimes mediators will organise family sessions where the whole family attends. At those sessions children are listened to, their loss acknowledged and needs expressed.

If your mediation is successful you will have achieved a separation quickly and without needing to spend a lot of money on lawyers. Sometimes mediation has the added benefit of changing how you and your ex relate to each other; your relationship may have been like a war and your mediator has come in as a peacekeeper. If new issues arise and you have confidence in your mediator, go back to him or her for additional sessions if you need to. It's better than letting disagreements and resentments fester and grow into full-blown conflict.

Collaborative Law

A lawyer called Stuart Webb practising in Minneapolis in the United States developed the idea of collaborative law in the early 1990s. He decided he was fed up with the way divorce law was practised (the traditional adversarial model) and he told his clients that he wouldn't go to court anymore. He said he would help them settle and negotiate their divorce outside the courtroom with lawyers who were similarly minded. If that didn't work and they wanted to go to court at a later date he would withdraw and hand the case over to another lawyer.

Other lawyers followed his thinking and they then came up with the idea of signing a four-way contract between the lawyers and the parties. They would all agree to negotiate honestly and in good faith and the lawyers would agree to help them settle their cases with as little conflict as possible. The lawyers also said that they would withdraw from the case if the parties couldn't settle and wanted to go to court.

In practice this means that if you engage a collaborative lawyer he or she will represent you, work with other third-party professionals such as accountants, valuers and child psychologists, and assist you in roundtable negotiations with your ex to come to an amicable settlement. It also means that if you decide at the end of a number of sessions that it's not working and you can't settle that you'll have to hire a new lawyer.

Both sides have to be committed to the process. There has to be a good deal of honesty and trust for the process to work. If there are conflicts around parenting then child psychologists, therapists and other experts can become involved. If there are financial issues that need to be resolved valuers, accountants or forensic accountants can be hired and assist the process by providing neutral advice or opinions.

If negotiations break down irrevocably then both sides will have to hire a fresh team of lawyers if they decide to litigate through the courts. This threat in the background puts you and your ex under pressure to settle. If you have invested time and money in the collaborative law process you are probably more likely to want it to work and you certainly both won't want to go to the expense of hiring a whole new set of lawyers.

The lawyer's role is different in collaborative law cases. He or she has to advise clients on their legal position but also act in a creative and collaborative manner. It requires lawyers to be honest and open on your behalf, identify your broader interests, listen to your emotions as well as the facts, refrain from being adversarial and act cooperatively. In the end they must respect your decision and try to keep peace between you and your ex and make your children's interests central.

If it is successful it can help protect your children, friends and family from the fallout from your conflict and save you from the stress, time and money involved in litigation.

Collaborative law focuses on 'interest-based bargaining' rather than the old-style 'position-based bargaining'. Interest-based bargaining means that the lawyers try to discover the underlying needs, interests and concerns of the parties and their children and urge them to communicate with each other. Position-based bargaining is where both parties come to the table with a wish list and beat each other down from their positions until they meet somewhere in the middle.

Collaborative law means that both sides have a team representing them for the purpose of assisting them to negotiate and settle. It focuses on resolving the dispute and it is not therapeutic, but can have the effect of lowering your stress because you don't have to go through the court system. You still have to hire a lawyer, go to meetings, gather evidence, negotiate and try to settle your issues but you don't have the pressure of court dates or the possibility of a judge taking decisions out of your hands.

Collaborative law makes sense if you are aware that the vast majority of cases settle before they go to court. Unfortunately, the threat of a court date is often the only thing that will encourage people to settle their issues so without that looming in the background the issues may remain unresolved.

Both teams of collaborative lawyers will have an idea of what is fair in your particular circumstances based on their experiences of litigating similar cases through the courts. Your lawyer has a duty to represent your interests.

Collaborative Law in Ireland

In Ireland family lawyers mainly practise using the adversarial court system; however some lawyers have started using the collaborative law system here since 2005. Many of them have trained with Pauline Tesler, a well-respected teacher of the collaborative law method. She comes over to Ireland from San Francisco and runs workshops and training sessions for Irish lawyers, including lawyers who are with the Legal Aid Board. So if you are applying for legal services from the Legal Aid Board it is worth asking about collaborative lawyers if you and your ex are both interested.

There is an Association of Collaborative Practitioners in Ireland and its website explains what collaborative law is and what it can do for you – information is in the resources section of the book. It lists practitioners and practice groups all over the country and explains how they operate. If you engage a collaborative lawyer they should charge you by the hour. Rates can vary hugely so you should always ask about rates and look for recommendations. How many sessions you need will depend on how complicated your case is and how well you get on with your ex.

Collaborative lawyers are usually solicitors, although barristers can become involved. If your case has complicated issues or you are worried about financial matters you can always ask your solicitor for a consultation with a barrister or an accountant or you can get a written opinion from a barrister who is an expert in family law.

It helps to have information that is accurate and up to date on legal matters and what generally happens when cases go to court. You are still trying to settle things fairly and the bottom line is that if you don't have any idea of what might happen in court it's hard to gauge what is fair, i.e. the ultimate decider in your case will potentially be a judge so it's useful to have an idea of what a judge might do in your particular case.

It's always hard to say what a judge might do (because different judges make different decisions) but a practicing family law barrister will have a better idea of what decisions are being made in court than a solicitor who doesn't litigate.

How Collaborative Law Works

If you decide to try collaborative law you would normally meet with a collaborative law practitioner for an initial consultation and at that time you should give him or her all the details surrounding your issues that need to be resolved. Your lawyer, your ex and his or her collaborative lawyer will then all meet together and have a few face-to-face meetings.

Everyone has to agree to work together to come up with the solutions to your issues. Other experts or expert opinions can become involved at these meetings. If you want to save time and money using this process you ought to gather as much information as possible before you meet your lawyer (see Chapter 4 on hiring a lawyer) and you ought to have a very clear idea of what issues you want to resolve.

If the process works, you can then have a document drawn up and used as a separation or divorce agreement. A judge may still need to be satisfied on certain facts or issues when you are getting your final order for a divorce or a consent order in court in relation to financial matters, maintenance, custody or access. Your lawyer should be able to advise you so that if you have to go to court to have your agreement made into a court order, or to have your divorce finalised, everything runs as smoothly as possible.

If the collaborative law process breaks down and you can't agree anything with your ex you will have to go to the trouble and expense of hiring another lawyer. The work you have done with your collaborative lawyers might have helped you narrow down your issues or given you an idea of where the conflict lies. So when you go to your new lawyer (who will help you get to court) you can give him or her very clear instructions.

Many separation and divorce cases in Ireland are settled at the door of a courtroom because you will both bargain as closely as you can to what you both perceive as fair on the day your case is due to be heard. Your barristers and solicitors will all prefer if you settle if they think you're both getting a fair deal. If one of you is making a low financial offer or keeping the other from having reasonable access to your children your lawyers will advise you to let the judge decide.

Collaborative law is a good idea if you know that you're getting a fair deal. Your lawyers should protect you from doing anything that is against your and your children's interests. If you are in any doubt as to the fairness of the negotiations or your case is not suitable for the ADR process then you ought not to use the collaborative law method.

Counselling

Many couples go to counselling when their relationship is in crisis. If your marriage or relationship has ended you can also go for counselling with the intention of discussing the issues that are causing conflict post break-up. You won't be going for 'couples' counselling' for the purpose of getting back together (although that can happen); you will be going for 'separation counselling'.

If you decide to use a counsellor for the purposes of resolving post break-up disputes make sure you are clear with your counsellor that that is your intention and that your counsellor is trained to help in a post break-up situation. Counselling is not the same as mediation but you may attend a counsellor who is trained in mediation so be sure about the definition of the service you are looking for. Your counselling sessions won't give you a document that looks like a separation agreement or will help you form the basis for a separation agreement but hopefully they will help you improve your communication and make decisions together.

In Ireland there are no laws regulating counselling. The word 'counselling' is used to cover the activities of a broad range of individuals who act as counsellors, therapists and psychotherapists. There are professional bodies for different types of therapy, counselling or psychotherapy and within each type of therapy members follow different schools of thought or have different methods.

Psychology and psychotherapy are more regulated than general therapy, counselling or life coaching and most psychotherapists will have undergone rigorous training and will follow a particular approach or school of thought. Some psychotherapists are already trained as doctors or psychiatrists, and as such are able to offer medical help and prescribe medication as well.

There are counsellors or psychotherapists who operate as individuals or in a centre. Their standards are set through professional bodies that regulate themselves and accredit counsellors and psychotherapists. There is more information on the different professions and their professional bodies in the therapy, counselling and advice section in the first chapter of this book and in the resources section at the end of the book. If you search online most of these bodies will provide contact details for members who provide their services. You should check up on the type of counselling or therapy your counsellor or therapist offers for you as a couple. Different types of therapy suit different people.

Generally a counsellor who specialises in separation counselling is there to help you and your ex resolve conflict by giving you a space within which you can start a dialogue, communicate and look at your behaviour more effectively than you could on your own. If it works for the purpose of resolving a specific dispute then hopefully you will both start to communicate and cooperate on parenting and financial issues.

Many people go to separation counselling so they can improve their relationship with their ex, end their relationship on better terms, or learn to communicate and parent well together.

A good counsellor will help you both look at your communication styles and your areas of disagreement. It's a bit like holding up a mirror to your relationship and allowing you both to see more clearly where the conflict is and what is causing it. You or your ex may have been avoiding conflict or engaging in a pattern of behaviour that causes conflict.

The characteristics of your relationship that make it difficult for you both to resolve your issues when you break up stem from behaviour patterns that existed while you were together. Your relationship may have followed a pattern of conflict initiation by one person and avoidance by the other, or one of you may have been demanding communication and the other withdrawing over time.

A counsellor will intentionally form a relationship with you both and use his or her communication skills to help you to improve your relationship. Your relationship with your counsellor ought to be confidential and he or she should treat you both with respect and empathy. It helps if your counsellor has a style and personality that you are both comfortable with.

There are many different types of counselling and therapy. The following are a few types that are popular:

- Brief therapy – brief therapy is a solution-based therapy that focuses on a specific problem and the therapist works directively to make a specific intervention and for a limited number of sessions, for example if both parties had differences in parenting styles.

- Cognitive behavioural therapy (CBT) – therapists who use CBT look at your thoughts, emotions and behaviour and ask you to look at and assess the dysfunctional ways in which you behave.

- Imago therapy – couples are encouraged to talk directly to each other and mirror each other's dialogue so that each person's understanding of the other is deepened.

In Ireland there are lots of different counselling services. Some of them are government funded and some are private. Relationships Ireland (formerly the Marriage and Relationship Counselling Services) bases its fees on your ability to pay and the Family Support Agency (FSA) is a free counselling service funded by the government.

Some counsellors operate in practices with their colleagues in related areas and some operate on their own. If you are unemployed you may be able to avail of free counselling or a reduced rate with a student counsellor in a private practice.

4

Lawyers and Litigation

Introduction – Your family law case – The Legal Aid Board – Hiring a lawyer – Representing yourself – Interacting with your lawyer – Controlling your costs

Introduction

If your marriage, civil partnership, cohabitation, house-sharing arrangement or co-parenting arrangements have hit the rocks and none of the alternatives to litigation (negotiation, counselling, mediation or collaborative law) have worked and you need to hire a lawyer to deal with custody and access issues surrounding your children, living arrangements, property issues, debts and/or to settle your finances then unfortunately you're probably going to have a rough time.

You can go to court to settle your issues if you are in a relationship with issues that need to be settled. The family courts will hear your case if it is recognised by law as a particular type of relationship and fulfils certain criteria, for example if your relationship is recognised by law as a marriage or a civil partnership. Irish family law Acts (there are many laws that apply to marriage, relationships and families) and the recent Civil Partnership and Certain

Rights and Obligations of Cohabitants Act 2010 (the 2010 Act) recognise a wide range of relationships and the courts have the power to make orders to regularise your affairs post break-up if your relationship is recognised under the various acts. You can bring applications for remedies that are similar to separation and divorce proceedings if you are in a civil partnership or qualify as a cohabitant under the 2010 Act.

A civil partnership is like a marriage and you have certain rights and responsibilities under the 2010 Act, but civil partners have fewer rights than a married couple. Interestingly, you can dissolve a civil partnership more easily than a marriage (after two years).

If you live together and are recognised as a financially dependent cohabitant by fulfilling the criteria in the 2010 Act you can apply to court for certain orders. Your relationship qualifies if you are same sex or opposite sex adults who are not married and haven't registered a civil partnership but have been living together in an intimate and committed relationship for at least five years if you have no children and two years if you have children.

If you aren't in a relationship that is recognised by law but you have had a child by your partner then you are entitled by law to bring an application for maintenance. If you have bought a house with someone and your relationship isn't recognised by law then you can't seek remedies under any of the family law Acts or the 2010 Act. You must bring proceedings in the ordinary civil courts to regularise any outstanding financial disagreements and proceedings (usually called partition proceedings) to resolve your property issues.

No One Likes Going to Court

Going to court is a scary, daunting experience for people who have never been inside a courtroom. Even lawyers who spend lots of time litigating find it nerve-wracking. In Ireland, the practitioners in the family courts, the staff of the courts services and family law judges all do their best to make courtrooms as user-friendly and informal as possible but litigants still have to swear an oath or make an affirmation and face an intimidating courtroom, a lawyer who can cross-examine you and a judge who is going to make very far-reaching decisions about your life. The courtroom has its own procedures, language, dress code and schedule, all of which are confusing and deeply mysterious to non-lawyers.

The best person to explain how you should approach your litigation is your lawyer, and unless you have an inside track or an excellent, dedicated and patient lawyer you may end up frustrated, lost, distressed or confused.

No one enjoys the process of litigation and people who aren't happy with the progression of their cases continually look for advice from friends and other professionals as to how to deal with their lawyers. It may be that their lawyer isn't giving them the attention they need or they may be difficult clients themselves, but often it's the nature of the legal process that is to blame.

A courtroom isn't a nice place to go to resolve the end of your relationship. It would be much better if everyone could sit down around a table and have time to air all their issues with a team of mediators, finance experts, child psychologists and therapists, but we are living in the real world. If you cannot agree on your issues with your ex you will probably end up negotiating an agreement at the door of a courtroom or allowing a judge to make a lot of decisions about your future.

In reality, very few family law disputes actually make it to the stage where both sides get into the witness box, present their cases, give evidence and have a decision imposed by a judge. The vast majority of litigants settle their cases by negotiation after they have hired a lawyer or at the door of the courtroom on the day of their case. At that stage the issues have been narrowed, both sets of lawyers have a good idea of what would be a fair decision in all the circumstances and the parties are prepared to negotiate.

During the course of the day your case is due to be held your ex or his or her solicitor may make a settlement offer that buys off your risk inside the courtroom. You may refuse that offer and insist on going ahead. At that stage your decision-making power has gone and anything can happen.

If your case goes into the courtroom for a hearing then the decision-making power about your lives goes to a judge. You may have to do things you think are completely unfair at the end of your case – see less of your children, sell property, pay maintenance, move house or live on less income than you think you possibly can. All these decisions are outside your control once your relationship had ended because the ultimate decision maker if you can't agree your issues between yourselves is a judge.

As soon as you are married, have children or commit to a long-term relationship with another person you have entered into a situation where you may have to be involved in litigation whether you like it or not. You can't turn the clock back or avoid it. All you can do is try to manage the process in the best way you can. Sometimes you have to go to court because there is no way the issues in dispute can be negotiated or settled. If your ex refuses to consent to a divorce or separation, won't pay maintenance, denies you custody or access, acts violently towards you or has abused your child sexually, physically or psychologically, or has neglected or abducted your child then litigation is probably inevitable.

Your Family Law Case

The District Court, the Circuit Court and the High Court

The District Court

The District Court is the busiest of all the family law courts. You can't apply for a judicial separation or a divorce in the District Court but you can make a lot of applications in relation to other family law issues. The District Court can deal with any proceedings relating to domestic violence, guardianship, paternity tests, custody and access by parents and grandparents. It can also make orders for maintenance for up to €500 per week for a spouse and up to €150 per week for a child or a lump sum up to €6,348.69.

Your case will be heard by a judge and in private. Only you and your lawyers will be allowed to attend unless the judge rules otherwise. You can apply for quite a broad range of orders in the District Court and there are no court fees payable in family law proceedings.

The proceedings in the District Court are usually started by a summons which has the names of both parties, the claim being made and the date and location of the court where the summons will be heard. There are rules and time limits in relation to how you serve the summons on your ex and you ought to look at the District Court Rules online or ask your lawyer or the District Court registrar for information so that the summons is properly served.

If you can afford it it's a good idea to get a solicitor or barrister to represent you in the District Court if the implications of the order are very serious. If you qualify for legal services from the Legal Aid Board it will be less expensive than paying for a private solicitor or barrister but if you don't qualify for legal services it can be very expensive to hire a legal representative for the day.

If you are making an application to the District Court on your own you can make an appointment to see the registrar of the court. The registrars are civil servants who work for the Department of Justice. They are responsible for the running of the court, drawing up orders and helping the judge. They have a huge amount of knowledge and can be very helpful at explaining the system to potential litigants and helping them to prepare their applications. It is not their role to give legal advice.

In the District Courts some judges act in a very informal manner before hearing a case. They may ask the litigants questions and behave like mediators and help the parties to negotiate. This can be very helpful (and unexpected) for litigants.

If you are not happy with the decision of the District Court you can appeal the decision to the Circuit Court and you will get a full re-hearing. After that you can't appeal again except on a point of law.

The Circuit Court

If you are seeking a divorce or a judicial separation or a higher amount of maintenance than is available in the District Court (there is no limit to the amount of maintenance that can be awarded in the Circuit Court) then your case has to be heard in the Circuit Court and you will face a longer waiting period before your case reaches a stage where it can be settled or heard by a judge.

Litigants who are seeking a divorce or judicial separation will often hire solicitors but some litigants represent themselves. If you have hired a solicitor he or she will usually start by having a consultation with you to gather information and then start things rolling by sending a letter to your partner or spouse or his or her legal representative. By law your solicitor is obliged to discuss with you the possibility of reconciliation, mediation and negotiation and to give you a list of mediators. If the issues can't be dealt with consensually then your solicitor will draft family law proceedings (family law civil bill, affidavit of means, affidavit of welfare and notice to trustees), which are documents that will be lodged in the court offices.

The proceedings are formal legal documents that set out the facts of your case and the orders you are looking for from the court. There are rules as to how the proceedings ought to be served on your ex – the rules are different if he or she lives abroad – and your lawyer ought to make sure that all the proceedings are properly served.

Your ex may or may not reply to your proceedings by putting in an appearance or lodging a defence during the specified time periods and this can delay the start of your case. If he or she decides not to defend the proceedings then your case will be heard anyway with or without your ex being present in court.

Before your case is ready to be heard you may need to get documents and information yourself or seek documents or information from your ex in relation to the issues in dispute.

Your case may require documents or expert witnesses to provide evidence that is relevant to your case. The court may require evidence of both your incomes from an accountant or your employers, information in relation to the willingness of banks to lend you money, a valuation of the family home from an auctioneer and a psychologist's or GP's report in relation to you or your children. Getting the relevant information, documents and reports takes time and you will need to make sure that you are on top of things as well as making sure your ex, your solicitor and other professionals are preparing their documents efficiently.

The court will monitor the progression of your case by issuing you with a summons to appear before the county registrar. The registrar will make sure that everything that is needed to progress your case is being done so that your case can be dealt with speedily and efficiently.

When all the documents, evidence, proceedings and witnesses are organised and your case is ready to go you will be given a date for the hearing. On that date you will meet with your legal team and your ex will meet with his or her legal team and you will either negotiate and settle your case or have your case heard by a judge.

Cases are sometimes adjourned on the day they are meant to be heard for many different reasons and you should be prepared for this to happen. If the list of cases for the day is very long your judge mightn't reach your case, or a vital witness might be unable to attend. A judge may also part hear a case and adjourn it to another date for an update or further information if he or she thinks that is appropriate.

If you aren't happy with the decision of the Circuit Court then you can appeal it to the High Court for a full re-hearing. There's no further right of appeal except on a point of law.

The High Court

The High Court has the power to hear family law cases but very few family law cases come before it as they are normally dealt with in the Circuit Court. If the rateable valuation of your family home exceeds €252.95 you may opt to have your case heard in the High Court. Cases come before the High Court if the parties are very wealthy and their income and assets are worth a lot or if their case is particularly complex. If you appeal from the High Court your appeal will be heard in the Supreme Court.

Different Rights and Remedies for Different Relationships

The legal system in Ireland recognises different relationships in different ways. You have more rights and remedies if you are married than if you are in a civil partnership or a legally recognised cohabiting relationship under the Civil Partnership and Certain Rights and Obligations of Cohabitants Act 2010 (the 2010 Act). You have fewer rights and remedies if you are unmarried or your relationship isn't recognised because you haven't lived together for very long or you have no children together. If your relationship doesn't fall under any of the relevant family law headings then you will have to sort out your disagreements through the ordinary civil courts. You will be able to sue your ex in the ordinary civil courts in the same way as you would be able to sue a business or individual for unpaid debts or seek partition proceedings for the division of a jointly owned property.

Marriage

If you want to put the end of your marriage on a formal footing there are five different ways to separate which are detailed below:

- Judicial separation: If you apply for a judicial separation this means that you are going to live apart and make formal arrangements for your separate lives. An application for a judicial separation must be based on one of the following grounds: unreasonable behaviour, adultery, living apart for one year where both parties agree to the separation, living apart for three years where one or both parties agree, or where the court considers that no normal marital relationship has existed for one year. Judicial separation proceedings allow you to apply for a huge range of orders to regulate your lives post separation, including financial adjustment orders, maintenance, property, custody and access orders.

- Divorce: If you apply for a divorce and are granted an order this means that your marriage is over and you can remarry. The grounds for divorce are that the parties must have lived apart for four of the previous five years, have no reasonable prospect of reconciliation and proper provision must have been made or will be made for the spouses and any dependent members of the family. As part of your divorce you can apply to incorporate a previous judicial separation or separation agreement. You can also apply for all the other orders you need to arrange your separate lives.

- Separation agreement: A separation agreement is an agreement where a married couple (or couples in other types of relationships) agree to live separately. It can be made at any stage by a separated couple and no reasons are needed. It usually incorporates an agreement to live apart and can incorporate agreements in relation to custody and access of children, financial matters, taxation and succession rights. You can make a separation agreement on your own, with your solicitor(s) by negotiation or by mediation with a mediator.

- Barring orders: A barring order which excludes your spouse or partner from your home is a way of bringing a relationship to an end. It doesn't make you officially 'separated' by law but it is used by many litigants in the

District Court as a way of formally ending their relationship. There is more information on barring orders in the section on domestic violence in Chapter 6.

• Annulment: If you think your marriage never validly existed or you have grounds for an annulment then you may also decide to seek a decree of nullity. The law of nullity is dealt with in Chapter 6.

Civil Partnership

In January 2011 a registration scheme was introduced for same sex couples. Couples who register under the scheme have rights and obligations towards each other that are similar to the rights and obligations of married couples. The laws in relation to children have not changed so a civil partner can't apply for guardianship, adoption, maintenance, custody or access to a child because of their registered relationship. Under Irish law at present only natural parents and heterosexual couples can have comprehensive rights and obligations in relation to children. If a couple who have registered a civil partnership wish to put the end of their relationship on a formal footing they can dissolve their partnership (similar to a divorce), draw up a separation agreement or seek a decree of nullity in the same way as married couple might do. There are some differences:

• Dissolution: A decree of dissolution of a civil partnership allows both parties to marry or enter into another civil partnership. If you want a decree of dissolution both parties must have been living apart from each other for a period amounting to two out of the previous three years before the application is made. The court must also be satisfied that proper arrangements have been made or will be made for both civil partners. You must submit two documents to the Circuit Court – a family law civil bill and a statement of means.

- Separation agreement: A couple who have entered into a civil partnership can draw up a separation agreement between them with or without the help of their lawyers.

- A barring order: You can seek a barring order under certain circumstances (see Chapter 6).

- Annulment: Nullity of a civil partnership means that a valid civil partnership never existed. The law of nullity is different for civil partnerships than for marriages and is dealt with in Chapter 6.

Cohabitation

Cohabitants are defined in the 2010 Act as two same sex or opposite sex adults who are not married to each other, not registered as civil partners (but could be) and are living together in an intimate and committed relationship for at least five years, or two years if they have a child together. If a couple qualify as cohabitants under the 2010 Act they do not have the same rights as married couples or civil partners but they do have some rights including property rights, and rights and duties in relation to their children, adoption, fostering, inheritance, maintenance and access to fertility services. If you are part of a recognised cohabiting couple and your relationship breaks down then you can apply for redress through the redress scheme for cohabiting couples:

- Redress: Usually you should apply for a redress order within two years of the end of your relationship. When the court makes a decision it takes into account the financial circumstances, needs and obligations of the cohabitants, the rights of others (former spouses, former civil partners and dependent children), the duration and nature of the relationship and the contribution of each cohabitant, financial and otherwise. The cohabitants can apply for orders such as maintenance orders, property adjustment orders, pension adjustment orders and attachment of earnings orders. They can also apply for provision to be made from the estate of their deceased cohabitant. You have no automatic right to get these orders. The court will make the orders if it is satisfied that you were financially dependent on your cohabitant partner.

- Voluntary agreements: Cohabitants can make voluntary agreements on financial matters but they may be regarded as valid only if each cohabitant has had legal advice or waived the right to legal advice, the agreement constitutes a contract and the agreement has been signed by both.

- Barring order: You can seek a barring order against your cohabitant in certain circumstances (see Chapter 6).

Presentation of Your Case

If you have to present your case before a judge (either with or without a lawyer) you should:

- Stand up when the judge enters the courtroom. If you have to address the judge call him or her 'Judge'.

- Try to speak up clearly and direct your answers to the judge – not your ex, your lawyer or your ex's lawyer.

- Dress appropriately. It doesn't give a good impression to a judge if you look scruffy. Even if you are in financial difficulty you can still look clean and neat.

- Tell the truth. It's amazing how obvious it becomes when a lie is being told in court. Good barristers and judges are almost psychic when it comes to spotting lies, so don't even think about it. If you don't know the answer say, 'I don't know' or 'I can't remember' and explain why. Perhaps you never had the information or it was a long time ago.

- Listen to everything your ex says in the witness box and if necessary take notes. If he or she is telling lies then you ought to communicate this to your solicitor and barrister if you think they don't know. Your ex must be cross-examined in relation to things he or she says that are untrue so that you can put forward your side of the story later if necessary.

- Don't lose your temper. Even if you are furious and your ex has told a pack of lies be patient. Answer the questions put to you by your barrister or the judge calmly, think about what you are saying and take your time. The courtroom is there for you to have your say and present your case so make sure you use your opportunity fully.

- If the process is unbearably upsetting or distressing for you then ask the judge for a break.

- Listen to the advice you are given by your lawyers; there is usually a reason behind it. For example, if you are under cross-examination from your ex's legal team you aren't allowed to talk to your legal team. There may be specific issues or information that you can't disclose or make part of your case for legal reasons. Ask your lawyers to explain to you why you can or cannot do something so that it makes sense to you.

- Don't interrupt the judge, your lawyers or your ex while they are talking.

- If you're put in the horrible situation of being cross-examined by an abusive ex who is representing him or herself, make sure that you are prepared for it, remain calm and be aware that judges are very experienced – they will have seen this before and will not appreciate their courtroom being used to abuse you.

The Legal Aid Board

Litigation is expensive. Unless you qualify for legal services (heavily subsidised legal advice and representation) from the Legal Aid Board you will have to pay the full cost of hiring a lawyer for advice and representation. If you want to apply for legal services you must go to the Legal Aid Board. The Board has financial eligibility limits. In order to qualify for legal services from the Board you have to satisfy a means test in relation to your income and assets. You must also pass a merit test, which means that the Board will not grant you legal services unless it is satisfied that your case is legitimate and one that a reasonable person would be advised to take.

The Legal Aid Board is an independent body and it was set up for the provision of legal services, i.e. legal advice and legal aid for persons of 'modest means'. Legal advice is any oral or written advice, including letters and negotiations, given by a solicitor or a barrister. Legal aid is representation in court proceedings by a solicitor or barrister.

There is an explanation of how the means test works on the Legal Aid Board's website (full contact details for the Board, its website and its local offices are in the resources section at the back of the book) and it changes from time to time, so the best thing to do is to check it out online or make an appointment at your local office. There are many local offices around the country so you ought to check the Legal Aid Board's website or telephone the Board to find your nearest office. At the time of writing, in order to qualify for legal services from the Board you have to show that your annual disposable income is less than €18,000. Your capital resources (property excluding your home, cars, investments cash, and any other resources that has a value) are taken into account when assessing financial eligibility. Allowances are given for certain debts such as credit union or bank loans; these may be offset against capital. If you have more than €320,000 in resources you don't qualify.

The Board calculates your disposable income by taking your gross income and making deductions of certain allowances. At the time of writing the allowances are as follows:

	Maximum amounts
Dependent partner/spouse	€3,500
Adult and child dependants (per dependant)	€1,600
Accommodation costs	€8,000
Childcare per child	€6,000
Income tax	full amount
PRSI	full amount
Ex gratia payments to applicant	€1,040

Child Benefit (and certain other payments) is not regarded as income. The Board will require documentary evidence and can request the Department of Social Protection to investigate your means when you apply for legal services.

Don't rely on the above information because it can change. Make sure you check on the up-to-date eligibility limits if you intend to apply to the Board for legal services.

If you qualify for legal services you will have to pay a contribution to the Board. At the time of writing you make a contribution of between €10 and €150 for a consultation for legal advice depending on your level of disposable income.

If you wish to go to court and you need legal services then you have to pay a contribution towards the cost of those services. There is a complicated (but fair) formula that the Board uses to work out what your contribution should be. It may be as little as €50 or it may be several thousand Euro, depending on your income and capital assets.

The level of the fee you pay as a contribution may also relate to the actual cost to the Board of providing you with the legal services. You ought to apply to the Board for legal services if you are unsure if you are eligible or not and ask the Board to assess your eligibility and the contribution that you will have to pay. Make sure you are organised and go to any meetings with the proper documentation and evidence required by the Board.

If your financial circumstances change you have to inform the Board of the changes. If you recover money or property at the end of your case the Board may seek to recover the costs of providing you with their services from you.

There are local law centres in every county, some are open part-time and some are open full-time so you need to check opening hours. The waiting periods for appointments vary, but the Board aims to ensure that if you are eligible you will get an appointment within four months from the time your application is completed. If there are special circumstances surrounding your case you may get an earlier appointment.

The Board has a mission statement, customer charter, complaints procedure and customer liaison officer. The members and staff of the Board are committed to providing a 'professional, efficient and cost-effective legal aid service'. So you should expect the best.

Hiring a Lawyer

You've heard all the horror stories. There are some bad lawyers out there. There are also a lot of excellent lawyers. How can you get the best?

Hiring the right lawyer is crucial. For defendants in criminal cases having the right lawyer can determine whether or not they end up going to jail or leaving court with their freedom. You are not going to get a perfect lawyer but it's important to get the best one you can afford.

If you're applying for legal services it's important to register yourself as soon as possible, as there may be a waiting list. So even if you're not sure whether you're going to need a lawyer from the Legal Aid Board or qualify under their criteria or not get on their list as soon as you suspect it may be necessary. There are other agencies that provide legal advice but will not represent you in court, such as the Free Legal Advice Centres. There are details in the resources section about the different organisations that offer free legal advice. Make sure you know the difference. There is no point in having an advisor who can't write letters for you or isn't willing or able to appear in court if you want to be represented on the day.

You should shop around before you hire your lawyer. As a potential client you should have an initial consultation with a few different solicitors before you pick the one to represent you. If you're getting legal services that are subsidised or free then you may not have a choice of solicitor. Even if it's free you should still be fussy. Having a bad lawyer can be worse than having no lawyer at all. So if you're not happy with what's available look for an alternative.

You should ask people you know and trust who have been through a separation or divorce which lawyer they used and what their experience was like. Remember that your style may be different to theirs. If you want to resolve everything amicably then there is no point hiring a 'Rottweiler'. If the conflict is high and you have to go to court there's no point in hiring a collaborative lawyer.

If you know people in the legal profession then you can ask them to recommend a good solicitor. They will know from firsthand experience what you need and who is good at family law.

Very big firms in Ireland can be excellent because they are well-resourced and have a large variety of experts, but they may be more expensive and impersonal than some of the smaller firms. Sole practitioners can provide a very efficient, dedicated and personal service so don't be too impressed by a big name.

Ask the firm or individual if they do a lot of family law. The internet isn't always accurate but it's worth Googling the name of the person or firm you are considering. Look at their website and see if they have experience in the area. Some lawyers lecture in family law or have written books on the area; this may make them good academics but not necessarily good negotiators. If your case is very complicated you might need an expert in a particular area – again you should ask around and check with others who have used that particular lawyer before.

Some of the most well-known names in family law are also incredibly expensive. You might be better to get a lawyer who has a good general practice and is tenacious and efficient. Sometimes lawyers get a reputation for being an expert in an area and are extremely busy. There can be a danger that they may have too much work going on and cannot give your case the attention it deserves.

Treat hiring a lawyer with the care you would exercise if you were hiring an employee who is going to be in your life for a few years.

If your case is going to the Circuit Court you will probably need to hire a barrister as well as a solicitor. Most people don't know the difference between the two professions so below is a simple explanation of how the differences apply in family law cases.

A *solicitor* works in an office (usually with a secretary) as a sole practitioner or in a partnership with a number of other solicitors. You can call up and make an appointment to see him or her and have an initial consultation. If your case is fairly simple and you just need them to draw up a separation agreement that you have already agreed then they will deal with your case themselves. If your case is set for hearing in the District Court then you should have a solicitor who is experienced at appearing in court representing you, or a barrister.

If you need to negotiate and it is straightforward then your solicitor may also deal with this. Your solicitor will be responsible for all correspondence that is sent between you and you ex. This correspondence will usually be sent to the solicitor representing your ex if he or she has one.

If your case is more complicated or contentious, if it needs an opinion from an expert or has to be negotiated or heard in the Circuit Court then you will need a very experienced solicitor who is used to appearing in the Circuit Court (there aren't many solicitors who do this) or a solicitor and a barrister. The *barrister* will receive a brief from your solicitor with all the details of your case and he or she will draft proceedings and affidavits, negotiate on your behalf and advise on legal aspects of your case. He or she will represent you in court if the case proceeds to full hearing. Most cases don't proceed to full hearing and are settled by negotiation before the court date or at the door of the court on the court date.

If you know you are definitely going to need a barrister then the same hiring rules apply. Insist on an initial consultation with your solicitor and barrister long before you go to court because you really don't want to meet someone on the day who has the wrong information about your case. You may have to pay to have this meeting but I believe it's worth it. If the barrister isn't up to speed with your case at that meeting, or you are not happy with him or her, ask your solicitor for a different barrister.

Call your solicitor's office a few days before the case and make sure that your barrister or solicitor isn't double-booked. If someone turns up at the last minute to take over your case and you strongly feel that he or she isn't up to speed then insist on an adjournment. Don't go ahead or be railroaded into accepting representation you're not happy with.

Representing Yourself

You have the option of not hiring a lawyer at all and representing yourself. In general this is not a good idea. You may not present your case in its best light and although the judge will be very helpful he or she may be constrained by time or not have the resources to act as an investigator or lawyer for both sides so that a fair and comprehensive judgment can be reached.

Lots of litigants represent themselves in the District Court if they are seeking custody, access, guardianship, maintenance or barring orders or directions from the Court. People represent themselves because they don't qualify for legal services or they don't want or can't afford to pay a lawyer.

If you are dealing with one simple issue and you are confident and knowledgeable about what you are doing then it can make sense in some circumstances to represent yourself. Similarly, if you are applying for an order that your ex consents to it may not be necessary to hire a lawyer. For example, if your ex is continually late to pick up your child for an access visit and it's driving you crazy you might decide to go on your own to the District Court and ask the judge for directions on the matter. If you have some legal knowledge you have managed to pick up yourself and you are fairly articulate then don't rule out representing yourself. Some solicitors will actually advise you to go into court on your own if the matter is a simple issue.

Judges will go out of their way to help if you are representing yourself. They will take the time and trouble to explain the system to you and try to be as fair as possible. On the whole they do prefer if both people are represented as it means the case is well prepared and that proceedings, valuations, reports, communications and negotiations are all documented and prepared by professionals.

Don't bury your head in the sand:
When that letter comes in the door, you are served with legal proceedings or you realise that you have no other avenue left open to you except recourse to law do not ignore the situation.

Answer that letter, hire your own lawyer or put in an appearance to the proceedings. Don't bury your head in the sand and hope it will all go away. The chances are that it won't and you will be at a disadvantage because you are unprepared or the judge in the case will be annoyed with you for ignoring his or her orders. You may well be penalised financially by obliging your ex to chase after you for appearances, information or meetings. Don't bin that official-looking letter. Deal with it as soon as you see it. It will cause you less trouble in the long run.

It's a bad idea to be ignorant about what's going on and to leave all matters in the hands of your lawyers. The more effort you put into your case the better it will go for you. Facts and nuances can easily get lost in communications, so the more directly involved you are in your own case the better. Often glaringly obvious and important parts of a case can be omitted because something was left out of a brief by mistake. Human error will occur and if you are on hand and alert to what is going on you can correct the things that will inevitably go wrong.

It is incredibly unfair that you have to go to the time, trouble and expense of hiring a solicitor to deal with a problem that you think wasn't of your creation, but that is life. No one ever said that everything in life was fair. You can always try to answer the letters yourself or ask a knowledgeable friend to give you a hand but make sure you answer those letters, instruct your solicitor to reply promptly to proceedings, appear on court dates and obey the directions of the court. To do otherwise is against your own interests. You are not dealing with the matter efficiently to facilitate your ex. You are dealing with it efficiently so that your interests are well represented.

Educating yourself about the process of litigation does not mean that you have to go out and get a law degree. It's a good idea to read a chapter on family law in a basic legal textbook or to look on one of the websites suggested at the end of this book. You don't want to be completely in the dark. Handing your fate over to anyone in complete ignorance, whether it is a doctor, lawyer or financial advisor, is never a good idea.

Interacting with Your Lawyer

Your lawyer will ask you to gather information that is relevant to the issue that is currently being dealt with. Lawyers are often handed diaries, long handwritten descriptions or reams of financial records that are impenetrable and irrelevant. If you want to gather the best information possible for your legal proceedings then you must keep it comprehensive and to a minimum. A valuation need only be one page long. Financial records, pay slips, tax returns and expenses should be summarised, stapled together and vouched in date order. Try to make it really easy for your lawyers to understand what you are giving them.

If you are having a row about the division of assets or income you will need to have a list of the relevant assets and income prepared. You may need up-to-date valuations, pay slips, bank account balance details, credit card bills, details of household expenses and pensions and everything else your lawyer or accountant tells you is relevant.

Keep everything in separate folders. Label everything. Do a one-page synopsis of the relevant information. Make it as easy, clear and accessible as possible. Type it up. Don't hand your solicitor a big bunch of documents in a box. He may go through it but it will cost you and there may be errors or omissions that only you know about.

Hire an accountant or an auctioneer/estate agent to value your property, business or other assets. You may be able to agree on valuations with your ex on some of these matters and if so write everything down and sign off on the agreed valuations. Don't do anything verbally. It's not a great idea to walk into court and say that the house next door went for €400,000 – this is not sufficient evidence of the value of *your* property.

Your solicitor and/or barrister should guide you on what evidence you will need to prepare for mediation, negotiation or a fully fought court case. Follow their advice to the letter. They are the experts and they will tell you what is needed.

Some things are relevant and some are irrelevant. For example, if the behaviour of your ex is an issue then of course you ought to keep a record of any incidents. If you are seeking a barring order you ought to keep a diary of the events that are leading you to seek the barring order, relevant medical records, police complaints and relevant witness statements.

Ask your solicitor if the behaviour of your spouse is an issue. If it is not then keep the details of your marriage break-up – the affairs, lack of sensitivity and bad habits – to a minimum. Your solicitor may just need to know why the relationship broke down and that's all. If you want to rant on about your ex's nastiness for two or three hours then phone a friend or hire a therapist. It will be cheaper than spending two hours doing it with your legal team.

When it comes to settlement meetings or court dates make sure you dress well and are punctual. Bring along a friend or family member for support if you need to. Take a settlement meeting seriously. You may do well to negotiate early and not have to endure years of uncertainty and stress. However, you shouldn't be a pushover either and if you have good lawyers they will advise you not to settle if they feel it is unfair. Take their advice; after all you are paying for it.

If you have to appear in court and are going to be questioned by a barrister representing your ex do not under any circumstances tell a lie. It is amazing how the scrutiny of a barrister cross-examining a witness can show you up to be a liar even if your lie was inadvertent. You should keep your answers short and to the point. If you don't know something or you can't remember something then you ought to say 'I don't know' or 'I can't remember' rather than guessing or making something up. Judges are impressed by witnesses who are clear, concise and honest, and who don't whinge. If you appear reasonable in what you are asking for then you have a much better chance of obtaining it.

On the whole the system works fairly. Of course everyone on both sides walks away thinking they could have done better. Lawyers say that it is the sign of a good decision or settlement if both parties are unhappy.

Controlling Your Costs

Fees are a big problem for individuals caught up in the legal system. It's very expensive to hire a legal team and pay for expert reports, and the cost of photocopying, telephone advice and correspondence are shocking. In a wealthy country in an ideal world most people should be given subsidised legal services for family law cases and obliged to go to mediation information sessions before they hire a lawyer.

It's important to realise that lawyers make more money if your conflict level is high. Good, honourable lawyers will want you to settle your case as quickly, simply and fairly as possible. However, if you are having long, complicated and contentious litigation with your ex this will suit unscrupulous lawyers down to the ground.

The more correspondence, court dates, meetings and experts involved the more money for them. They won't care if you're fighting for years with your ex. The bill of costs will keep piling up and at the end of the day you may end up fighting over who will pay the legal bills or united in your hatred of your overpriced lawyers.

It's scary to think that a fight over who gets to live in the family home or who gets custody of children might cost you so much that no one gets to live in the house or you can't afford school trips, holidays or even college fees for your children. You could end up in a situation where the family home has to be sold to pay legal bills and your children are completely traumatised by the years of fighting it took to lose the house.

Be clear from the beginning. Before you pick up the phone be aware that every letter and phone conversation and each document, court date and application will cost money. Lawyers are professionals who have to pay expensive rent, overheads and support staff. They have many demands on their practice and it is expensive for lawyers to spend time on your case.

Your lawyer cannot be concerned with the minutiae of every detail of your separation or divorce. It doesn't make sense for him or her to get involved for hours and hours in a fight over who gets the wedding crockery or the flat-screen television. It may end up costing you more than those items are worth to involve your lawyer in trying to get them back for you.

At the same time, your lawyer isn't about to sit down with you and decide whether your son should be allowed to play computer games all day in your ex's home or walk home from school on their own to one house and not the other. These are problems that need to be dealt with in another way. There are government-funded professional mediators in the Family Mediation Service who can help you work out a parenting plan for free and their services should be availed of.

A lawyer will help you deal with overall macro-level issues during your separation or divorce. He or she can make sure orders are put in place that divide property and decide custody, access and maintenance. He or she is not there to help you humiliate your ex in the witness box.

Be aware that unless you qualify for legal services it's going to cost you to hire a lawyer. Don't presume that your ex will have to pay your legal fees or that you will get a lump sum at some stage to pay off the lawyers. It might actually be a good idea to work out a payment plan with your solicitor from the start so that you don't face a shocker of a bill five years later.

You ought to shop around if you think it is necessary. You might decide to consult with two or more solicitors. When you call up a solicitor make sure you are very clear on the phone. Ask to speak to the solicitor or his or her secretary and say the following:

'I would like to make an appointment for one hour to discuss a family law matter. I need to get a divorce/separation/issue proceedings for child custody/access or I need to defend proceedings.

Please let me know if there is a charge for this initial consultation. If there is a charge how much will that be?'

Some solicitors will charge for the initial consultation and some won't. It is important that you find out whether you will be charged or not before you go along for your appointment.

At the appointment you ought to explain the nature of your case and ask the solicitor what fees he or she might charge. It might be difficult at this stage for the solicitor to have an idea what the final bill of costs might be. If the case is very contentious and you need access to financial records and business records, or to hire forensic accountants or child psychologists, then the costs are going to be substantially more than a case that involves an employed couple on a fixed salary who own a house, have a joint bank account and two children in school. The complexity and contentiousness of your case will be the biggest factor in determining costs.

Keep a record yourself of every meeting, phone call and correspondence you have with your lawyer in relation to your case. Ask your lawyer for regular updates on the bill of costs. If your lawyer is reticent or vague about what the costs might be don't hire him or her. Lawyers have a legal duty to furnish you with a 'quote' for their services and they have to present their bill according to certain rules.

Solicitors base their fees and charges on on the following criteria: the complexity of the matter; the urgency of the matter; the difficulty of the questions raised; the skill, labour and specialised knowledge and responsibility involved; the number and importance of documents prepared or examined; the amount or value of any transaction involved; the importance of the matter to you; the time reasonably spent by personnel on the matter; and the place(s) or circumstances in which the matter is pursued.

A solicitor cannot charge you on the basis of a percentage of any award or settlement of your case.

Barristers base their fees on the nature and amount of work involved; the time involved in carrying out the work; the complexity, novelty or difficulty of the matter; the value and importance of the matter; the level of knowledge, skill and expertise required to deal with the matter; and the level of experience and expertise of the barrister. Barristers are obliged to give you a written estimate of their fees prior to undertaking work. Some lawyers will charge set fees for certain types of cases or give you an hourly or daily rate in advance.

If you are well off and have a house that's worth a lot of money and you both have great salaries don't be surprised if you get charged a lot more than a couple who own a small flat with a low income. Lawyers will charge more for cases that involve huge figures. There is more responsibility on the lawyers and more to lose if the assets are high worth. However, there is often the same amount of work involved in dividing assets worth €500,000 as there is in dividing assets worth €5 million.

Children from wealthy backgrounds need the same arrangements as children from less well-off families. So if you are well off you should be extra careful in relation to fees. Point this out to your lawyer. Ask them are they going to have to spend extra time on your case just because your house is more valuable or is your case quite simple and the fees are bigger because your property is worth more. It is worth paying higher fees if your lawyer is good and is going to save you money at the end of the day but make sure you know how your fees are going to be calculated.

Make sure you have an idea of what the potential costs might be. Your barrister will know how many days your case might run to. It would be unusual for your case to run for longer than a number of hours or days. Very complex medical negligence cases can run for weeks and some commercial cases can run for years and run up millions of Euro in costs.

Ask the solicitor and barrister during your consultation what the worst-case scenario might be. If your case is very complex you might need a senior counsel, who will be more expensive than a junior counsel. If you hire a senior counsel there will also be a junior counsel working on the team. This will cost a lot more and is only necessary in very few complex and difficult cases. An experienced junior counsel should be able to deal with a straightforward family law case.

Make sure you ask the right questions to cover every eventuality. You really don't want any nasty surprises. Ask if there is any chance of negotiating so that your ex pays some or all of the costs if he or she has more assets than you. If the case runs for three days how much will the barrister charge for each day? What will the solicitor charge? Do you really need a senior counsel as well as a junior counsel? Can you work out a payment plan? If the case goes very badly for you will you get a discount?

If at the end of the process you feel that your lawyers did a really bad job point it out to them and look for a reduction in your fees. If you're not happy with the bill or feel you are being cheated report the lawyer to his or her professional body – details of the legal professional bodies for solicitors and barristers are in the resources section at the back of the book.

5

Managing Your Finances

Introduction – Untangling your finances – Civil partnership and cohabitation under the new 2010 Act – What do the courts do? – Maintenance – Dividing your joint assets – Bankruptcy, mortgages and debt management – Budgeting – Living on less

Introduction

Back in the 1970s and 1980s in Ireland, when no one seemed to be fabulously wealthy, it was considered impolite to talk about money. Neighbours didn't boast about the value of their houses and no one ever asked you much you earned. During the so-called Celtic Tiger, property prices rose and Ireland experienced an economic boom that caused a change in attitude and people began to take a great interest in property and income. What you earned and what you owned became a common topic for discussion. It seemed as if everyone had a holiday apartment, and the country was full of property millionaires.

Many Irish people purchased their houses at the height of the property boom because they needed a place to live for themselves and their families and they thought that the property market was solid. These people are now stuck with large mortgages and negative equity.

Unemployment, cuts in public services and reduced pay packets have compounded the problem, and everyone is feeling the pinch.

The presence of the troika in Ireland and the hard-hitting recession have made the subject of money a very contentious topic. In the past credit and tax revenues were plentiful, the government spent to excess and Irish people were encouraged to borrow hugely and buy their houses at unrealistic prices. Now we're all paying on a macro level for the waste and bad decisions made by banks, politicians, regulators and speculators.

If you and/or your ex are having problems with your finances because of Ireland's economic problems then you will be feeling the financial pain on a micro level as well. There's no point in looking back at what you had or might have had. As a country and as individuals we have to try to negotiate our way out of the difficulties we face, learn from past mistakes and look forward as positively and optimistically as we can.

Achieving separate lives is expensive and some couples stay together because they can't afford to live apart or the reduction in their living standards would be too drastic and severe. If they have children they may not wish to lower their standard of living or plunge their financially stressed family into poverty. Sometimes there really is no option. Unless you are willing to move abroad, move home with your parents, lose your home, live in a hostel or lose contact with your children you may be unable to leave.

Couples who stay together for financial reasons only ought to go to counselling or mediation (individually or separately) for help to deal with the extreme stress and conflict that this situation can cause. It's helpful to acknowledge and talk about it because if it is ignored conflict can escalate, children can suffer and in extreme circumstances aggression and violence may ensue.

What Does Money Mean to You?

Money symbolises different things to different people. It may be survival, power, freedom, somewhere nice to live or regular holidays. For many of us, living in a capitalist society causes us to see our ability to earn money as part of our identity. Lack of money and huge debts can lead to depression or suicide. It's a powerful force in your life and it is well worth examining your relationship with money. If you are going to a therapist, it may be a topic of discussion for you.

Figure out what money means to you, why you want it and what you want to do with it. How important is money to you? Is it your reason for working? Look at yourself in the past. Were you a spender or a saver? Did you worry about money? Are you a gambler when it comes to investing your savings?

As we all have individual attitudes to money you may have had a different perspective on finance than your ex. During a marriage or long-term relationship couples have a financial as well as an emotional relationship. Their financial relationship can be healthy, highly dysfunctional or somewhere in between. Some couples are naturally financially astute. They make rational decisions, budget for the future and don't take risks. Other couples are careless spendthrifts who take chances with their money on stocks and shares they know little about and engage in risky property speculation. You may be part of a mismatched couple where one of you is careful and the other likes to take risks. Arguments about money can corrode relationships and are often the reason for a break-up.

Hopefully the collapse in the global markets has taught everyone in Ireland that small investors can't afford to speculate wildly. Your money is probably earmarked for your mortgage, living expenses, pensions and your children's education. Unless you're wealthy enough not to care about losing the money you invest in speculative ventures then you ought not to take risks. Putting your money in long-term capital guaranteed low-interest investments may be boring but it's safe. Maintain your house well and if you have it for a long time and didn't buy it for a crazy price then hopefully it will provide you with some security for the future.

Pre-marriage courses or relationship counselling can be an eye opener for couples who never discussed how they were going to manage their finances. If things go horribly wrong and you end up in serious financial difficulties you can turn to organisations such as the Money Advice and Budgeting Service (MABS) for help in managing your finances.

Without intervention many couples limp along with no real financial plan. Often one person takes total control of all the financial decisions because the other decides they're 'no good' with money. It's not a good idea to hand over all your financial power and decision making to your partner. You need to have an understanding of your family's financial picture. It is vital knowledge that you owe to yourself and your children. Who wants to wake up one morning to discover that everything you've both worked for is gone and you've lost your house and all your savings?

Untangling Your Finances

If you are organising your finances separately post break-up you should examine what your financial relationship was like during your relationship and decide how you want to move on from there in the future.

If you or your ex was horribly mean or a crazy gambler during your relationship then separating can give you a chance to regain some control over your own finances and re-establish your own financial mindset. If you or your ex has lost your job then the dynamic will have changed.

Look back at your relationship and think about your role in relation to your joint finances. Ask yourself the following questions:

- Do you have full knowledge of your joint financial relationship? Knowledge is power and lack of knowledge is dangerous. If the main earner in your relationship has no life insurance or there's no mortgage protection you could be in for a severe fall if your ex dies. If your joint savings are in a risky fund you might not have any pension provision for yourself in the future. If you have no house insurance and your house burns down you could end up homeless. Don't close your eyes and hope it will all work out okay – find out the position of your joint finances. Get on the phone to the bank, pension provider, accountant, mortgage broker, life insurance company and house insurance company and ask them all what's going on. It's scary but necessary to discover your true position. You may have been willing to leave all the financial matters in your ex's hands while you were together but now you have to take control. Your ex may be just as much in the dark about your true financial position as you are.

- Did you at any stage sit down and make decisions about how you were going to organise your joint finances? Unless you did a marriage course or sat down with a very proactive accountant or financial adviser then you probably never had a plan. Many couples just limp along, hoping that their partner doesn't spend too much and trying not to spend too much themselves. Your bills might have been on direct debit and if your earnings increased your spending probably did too. You may have had a few savings plans and a pension. Some smart couples budget and stick to it religiously but I suspect they are the exception. Many financial decisions are made on an ad hoc basis. One person is designated as the financial expert in the relationship and takes responsibility for the bills and financial planning.

- Were you or your ex a financial control freak? Financial bullying is abuse but if you're hopeless with money and can't control your spending your partner might have taken financial control away from you for a good reason. If one person takes control of the finances for the good of you both then that can work well, but if you are denied access to your joint funds are you being disempowered? The idea of one partner doling out pocket money to the other is patronising and demeaning. Lack of trust and a power imbalance in relation to financial control can completely undermine a relationship.

- What is your financial history with your ex? Did you or your ex have assets or savings before you got together? What happened to those assets? Was it your house that you both moved into or did you use your ex's savings to buy a house? The person who owned a house, inherited money or had a larger income at the beginning or during the relationship can feel that they deserve more than their spouse or partner at the end, but if you go to court a judge won't necessarily allow this to happen.

- What is the nature of your relationship? If you are married, in a civil partnership or cohabiting you have certain rights in relation to your joint income and assets and certain responsibilities towards your spouse or partner that are protected by law. The aim of the law is to protect children, spouses and partners who are in a weaker financial position by distributing the family income and assets fairly.

- What income did you have during the course of the relationship? What work did you do at home during the course of the relationship? Look back over your relationship with your ex and think about the times you worked and the times your ex worked. Try to get an overall picture of how much of your income or savings you put into the family home and running of the household.

- If you didn't work outside the home during all or some of your relationship think about why you didn't. Were you looking after the house or children? Were you helping your ex with his or her business or being supportive in some other way, for example by caring for a relative? Draw up a timeline of your relationship and look at what you did during various time periods and try to find supporting documents if you need to – old pay slips or household bills: your bank might be able to help you if you need to go back over your accounts and see what your income and expenditure were at specific times.

Doing all of the above will help you get a better picture of where you are before you decide where you are going to go. It's also good to have these details clear in your mind before you go for counselling, mediation, legal, budgeting or financial advice.

If you've been in a long relationship the chances are your lives and your assets and incomes have joined together over time. You may own a house in joint names, have joint bank accounts, and be beneficiaries of each other's pensions or life insurance policies.

When your relationship ends you may want to keep some of these assets joined together and separate others. Some of your assets represent things that have emotional value to you. It may be possessions like furniture, pictures, electronic equipment, wedding presents, family heirlooms, cars or holiday homes. If you agree to separate and decide to live apart most of your assets will have to be divided up or transferred.

You can't live without food or shelter, so having a roof over your head and a basic income are vital. The legal basis for separation, divorce and dissolution of civil partnerships is that they are agreements or court orders aimed at giving you both a way of living apart from each other; therefore nearly all couples will live apart after divorce, separation and dissolution.

Civil Partnership and Cohabitation under the New 2010 Act

The strength of your position after a break-up will depend on your legal status. Family law gives more rights and responsibilities to you as a family if you are married. If you are in a civil partnership or defined as a cohabitant by law then you have rights and responsibilities that are less than those enjoyed by couples who are married. If you aren't married, are not in a civil partnership or don't qualify as a cohabitant then you have very few rights and responsibilities.

The new Civil Partnership and Certain Rights and Obligations of Cohabitants Act 2010 commenced on 1 January 2011. The new laws on civil partnership allow same sex couples to register their relationships with a registrar in Ireland and have a ceremony like a marriage. It also recognises the marriages of same sex couples who are married under similar laws in other countries. If you register under the new Act as a civil partnership you gain rights that are less than but similar to those of a married couple.

The new Act offers rights and protections to same sex couples. When you register your civil partnership you are allowed property and succession rights, joint treatment for tax purposes and pension entitlements, and you can avail of the law in relation to maintenance and domestic violence if the relationship breaks down. You can also dissolve your partnership after two years. There are no rights to adopt jointly or to have joint guardianship of children raised together. Tax and social welfare benefits for civil partners are nearly the same as married couples.

The new laws also change the rights and obligations for cohabitants in long-term relationships and strengthen the position of financially dependent cohabitants, especially those with children.

No dissolutions of civil partnerships have been granted by the courts because no one has been in a civil partnership for two years yet but the courts will probably be guided by previous decisions made in the family law courts.

To qualify as a cohabitant under the Act you must live together in an intimate and committed relationship, you can be both of the same sex or the opposite sex and you must not be in a functioning marriage or have an existing civil partnership. If you were married you must be living apart from your ex-spouse for four of the previous five years – in other words be entitled to seek a divorce but you need not be divorced.

If you qualify as a cohabitant under the Act and you have been financially dependent because of your relationship with your cohabitant then you will be allowed to apply to the court for redress. The court will take into account lots of different factors, such as the needs of former spouses and children. You must have lived together for five years prior to the break-up if you don't have children together or for two years or more if you do have children. The court can make a number of orders such as maintenance, property adjustment orders, pension adjustment orders and related orders such as attachment of earnings orders. You can also apply for a share to be made to you out of a deceased cohabitant's estate.

The Act has a lot of conditions in it that you need to satisfy before you will be given the status of cohabitant and the court must also look carefully and consider the needs of children, earning capacity of cohabitants, rights of former spouses, rights of former civil partners, the duration of the relationship and contributions to looking after the home before it makes any orders in relation to property or compensatory maintenance.

If your relationship has broken down and you think you may have rights as a cohabitant then you ought to seek legal advice from an experienced family lawyer.

What Do the Courts Do?

Division of Assets for Married Couples

There are no hard and fast rules about how your assets, income and property will be divided up if you have applied to court for a judicial separation or a divorce. If you can't negotiate an agreement then your case will end up before a judge. The judge will base his or her decision on your unique circumstances, the legislation and previous case law. When the court makes a decision on how to divide assets during judicial separation or divorce proceedings it must make 'proper provision for both spouses' out of the assets of the couple. This requirement arises out of the special protection given to marriage in the Irish Constitution.

The court will take many different factors into account. Judges have a huge amount of discretion in how they make their decisions so it's really hard for a lawyer to predict what exactly will happen in your case.

Cases are heard in camera (in private) so there isn't any statistical information in the public domain apart from some research by journalists and basic information given out by the Courts Services on their website. Different judges have different attitudes so don't be surprised if your lawyer can't be precise about what might happen in your particular case.

Judges must make decisions about what 'proper provision' is by looking at the guidelines in the Acts and previous case law. The guidelines that the court must consider when dividing assets are set out in law and are the following:

- The income, earning capacity, property and other financial resources of both of you

- The financial needs, obligations and responsibilities which you both have or are likely to have in the future

- The standard of living the family had in the past

- Your ages, the length of your marriage and the length of time you lived together

- If either of you have any physical or mental disabilities

- Contributions either of you have made to the welfare of the family in terms of income, property, financial resources, looking after the children or looking after the home

- How your earning capacity was affected by family responsibilities: did you impair your ability to earn in the future because you left paid work to look after the home or family?
- Any income or benefits you are entitled to by law
- Conduct of either of you that it would be unjust to disregard
- Your accommodation needs
- The value of any benefit (like a pension) that you would be entitled to if you both stayed married
- The rights of anyone else, including a new spouse

The courts in Ireland will not discriminate against a dependent spouse, won't try to give spouses equivalent lifestyles and only very gross and obvious misconduct by a spouse is relevant. Assets aren't divided equally – the court uses the principle of 'proper provision' for spouses and children, and lots of discretion is exercised by the trial judge in deciding how to divide up assets.

If you are a dependent spouse who relied on your spouse's income during your marriage because you stayed at home, played a supporting role to your spouse and minded the house and children then judges in Ireland accept that post divorce you will need somewhere to live and an income to live on.

If you and your ex are in the small category of people who have 'ample resources' – a legal term that describes a situation where there are a lot of assets available to the separating couple – then normally the dependent spouse of a lengthy marriage will be entitled to between one-third and half of the family assets. Judges are concerned to make 'proper provision' for the dependent spouse rather than dividing assets equally.

If you're both unemployed, on social welfare, have debts or have very few assets then there may be nothing to divide. You may both end up in financial difficulty post separation and divorce, as a judge isn't going to leave either of you with no income at all. Going to court isn't going to solve your financial problems. A judge can't award you an income if it's not practically possible. In some cases coming before the courts couples have joint debts and negative equity. This is particularly challenging and can lead to huge conflict if the debts have to be shared, especially if one person blames the other for the debts.

Another Bite of the Cherry

The courts are guided by case law that says that while there is no such thing in Irish law as a 'clean break' it is legitimate to aspire to having a clean break and it's a good idea to make a settlement that is certain and stable. For example, if you inherit a large property after separation or divorce then you shouldn't have to share it with your dependent ex-spouse if he or she was properly provided for at the time of your separation or divorce. The courts say that the standard of living of an ex-spouse should be related to the standard of living enjoyed during the marriage. If you go back to court you can't look at the changed circumstances of your ex if he or she has made a lot more money and say that you are entitled to a share. In other countries you get your orders at the end of your divorce proceedings and that is it – the litigation is over.

In Ireland the situation is different. You can always go back to court and try for another 'bite of the cherry'. If you are making a separation agreement with your ex your lawyer will probably advise you to put in a clause saying that the terms of the separation represent a full and final settlement of all your claims against each other. However, this clause doesn't stop the court interfering at a later date. If you decide to get divorced the court may change the terms of your separation agreement. If you are paying maintenance and you lose your job or income then you can go back to court and apply for a reduction of the amount you have to pay.

The courts will be fair about it and probably won't intervene in the following circumstances:

- If the settlement was recent
- If the settlement was reasonable or generous
- If your ex frittered away his or her settlement
- If the settlement was intended to be full and final

The courts might intervene in the following circumstances:

- If lies were told about assets at the time of settlement
- If some unusual, unforeseeable events occurred between the time of settlement and the time of judicial separation or divorce

The Irish courts think that a 'clean break' is desirable if the family has enough assets to achieve it and that certainty and finality at the end of legal proceedings is a good thing. Similar rules will probably apply to civil partnerships although they have not been tested yet. Civil partnerships do not have the same standards of protection as a marriage in the event of a break-up. Responsibilities to children and divorce settlements that were made prior to the civil partnership will be taken into consideration by the courts.

Prenuptial, Pre-Civil Partnership or Pre-Cohabitation Agreements

Prenuptial agreements are agreements or contracts between couples that are signed before they get married. This type of agreement can also be entered into by same sex couples before they register their civil partnerships. They would probably be called 'pre-civil partnership agreements'. Cohabitants who want to live together without having legal rights or responsibilities might also decide to sign a 'pre-cohabitation agreement'. This type of agreement sets out how assets will be divided if the marriage ends, the civil partnership is dissolved or the cohabitation ceases.

In Ireland lots of couples live together without getting married or registering a civil partnership because they know that if they do they will lose control over their assets. The laws in relation to cohabitants mean that you can lose control of your assets by living with a same sex or opposite sex adult in an intimate and committed relationship for a period of two years if you have children together and five years if you don't.

Anyone in Ireland can make a prenuptial or pre-civil partnership agreement or even an agreement in relation to the terms of their cohabitation, but the agreement can't automatically be enforced by law. However, the courts can look at these types of agreements and take them into consideration in the context of judicial separation and divorce proceedings and will probably take them into consideration during dissolution of civil partnership proceedings or proceedings for redress taken by cohabitants as long as the agreements were made honestly and fairly and the interests of both spouses, civil partners or cohabitants are looked after.

Marriage is protected by the Constitution and the courts must make 'proper provision' for both spouses before a judicial separation or divorce is granted. A study group set up by the Minister for Justice in 2006 recommended that prenuptial agreements be defined by law, incorporated into legislation and looked at in the context of judicial separation and divorce proceedings in the same way as separation agreements. At present the court can look at prenuptial agreements and enforce them if it considers them to be compatible with its other considerations. It can consider them at the time of a divorce or separation but it can't attach as much weight to them as it has to attach to other factors it obliged to consider by law.

If you're going to draw up and sign a prenuptial or other type of agreement and you want it to be as strong as possible then you should both provide each other with full disclosure of your assets, get independent legal advice and sign an acknowledgement that it is legally binding. You should also insert a periodic review clause and put in agreements in relation to maintenance, assets and custody in the event that you break up.

Maintenance

If you're married or in a civil partnership, or to a lesser extent a recognised cohabitant, your income is treated in a different way to other couples. A dependent spouse, partner or cohabitant has the right to look for maintenance. If you've brought up your children and looked after the family home, Irish law recognises that as a contribution to the family's general well-being and will expect you to continue to be maintained at some level.

If you are a civil partner you will be able to apply for financial relief post break-up but there's no mention in the

2010 Act of the position of children or dependants living with civil partners. Cohabitants can apply for compensatory maintenance under the redress scheme if they are economically vulnerable after being in a long-term relationship.

If you were in a relationship that doesn't qualify under the 2010 Act you cannot apply for maintenance for yourself during or after a relationship. You also don't benefit from succession rights, taxation and pension benefits, and social welfare and housing benefits.

Dividing Your Joint Assets

Assets are anything of economic value that can be converted into cash and income is a flow of revenue that you receive from your work or any other source. As a couple you will have built up your lives together and there may be many assets you own together or that the court can consider. You don't automatically get to keep anything for yourself but it's not practical to expect a judge to award you your ex's personal possessions or things of sentimental value or significance.

The main assets, income and related matters that you will need to think about and consider are the 'family home' or 'shared home' or property held by you both, the family income, your individual incomes from salaries or jobs, joint businesses or a family business, savings, pensions, holiday homes, stocks, shares, bonds, potential succession rights, tax benefits, social welfare benefits and personal possessions.

Decisions relating to large assets and income can be made by agreement, negotiation, using an alternative dispute resolution process or via the courts. If you make a decision to agree on the division of assets by using a particular method or forum remember that the method you use may end up costing more than the asset you are fighting over.

Don't go to court if the legal fees are going to cost you more than the monetary value of the asset. If your ex offers you a deal that is near to what you might achieve in court then you ought to take it. Going to court can take a great deal of time and exert a huge emotional cost. Figure out a range of what would make you happy and, unless you're being offered something way out of that range, don't fight over it.

Your Family Home or Shared Home

The 'family home' or 'shared home' is usually the biggest asset owned by a couple. A 'family home' is the term used in law for homes normally lived in by married couples and a 'shared home' is the term used in law for homes normally lived in by civil partners or cohabitants. Your home has huge emotional and financial significance and deciding who gets to have it transferred into their sole name, how much money is given by one person to the other to 'buy out' your home, who remains living there for a period of time, or whether to sell or let it is the biggest decision made in most break-ups.

It's a good idea to get legal and financial advice around the issue of who gets to continue to live in the family home or shared home or, if it is treated as an asset, how the asset is divided up. Some couples resolve the issue by one party buying out the other. The home can be sold and the proceeds divided, if there are any. Nowadays many couples are in negative equity and can't afford to sell their home. One person may be left with a debt rather than an asset so it is very important to get good advice around this issue.

Unless you are very well off, you will be constrained by what the banks will allow you to borrow, the market value of your home and your income. There may be nothing to divide up if your home is in negative equity and you may have to think about renting.

How the home is treated in law is very different depending on whether you are married, in a civil partnership or legally recognised as cohabitants.

If you are married then your home is defined as your 'family home' and is protected in law by the Family Home Protection Act 1976. If you are civil partners your home is defined as a 'shared home' in the 2010 Act. Your 'family home' or 'shared home' is defined as a dwelling where a married couple or civil partners ordinarily reside, and your spouse or civil partner cannot sell, mortgage, lease or transfer it without your written permission in advance, even if it is in his or her sole name.

When you're separating your spouse or civil partner can't do anything with the family home or shared home until you have reached agreement or, if you can't reach agreement, until a judge makes a decision for you. If a judge has to decide what will happen to the home then he or she will look at the family circumstances, especially the welfare of a dependent spouse or civil partner and any children, and then will say if one of you has the right to live in it for a period of time, or how your ownership is going to be divided up.

Sometimes a court will allow the spouse who lives with the children to stay in the family home until the children are finished full-time education, i.e. until the youngest child is 18 or 23 (if they attend a third-level college). This part of the legislation isn't mirrored in the 2010 Act for same sex couples. The court can also make an order excluding one spouse or civil partner from entering the family or shared home.

The court can make lots of different types of orders in relation to the ownership of the home. It can order the home to be sold and the proceeds divided in different proportions. It can order that the home be sold immediately or the sale deferred for a long period. It can order a transfer of names on the property, or if it is a tenancy it can transfer the tenancy.

Recognised cohabitants don't have the protection that spouses and civil partners have in relation to their home but they can apply for property adjustment orders under the 2010 Act if they take proceedings for redress after a break-up. Cohabitants have no automatic right to get such orders and the court must take into account the needs of both cohabitants and their former spouses, civil partners and children, the nature and duration of their relationship and the contribution made by both, either financial or otherwise.

If you are not married, in a civil partnership or cohabiting then you are in a different situation entirely. The home you live in is not protected by the Family Home Protection Act 1976 or the 2010 Act and you must be vigilant to protect your property rights. It's important to keep a good record of any mortgage repayments, financial contributions or improvements that you have made towards the property. You will need to look at how you decided to register your interest in your property. Are you joint owners or tenants in common? Joint owners own the property together – there's a presumption that you each own half of the property and if one person dies the other inherits it.

As tenants in common you each own separate shares of the property that may not represent half of the value of the property and those shares are part of your estate if you die, and don't necessarily go to your cohabitant. It's very important to get good legal advice about the title of your property as it can be quite technical, and if you need to take proceedings you must be sure that you are taking the right proceedings in the right court.

If you are living together and you decide to separate then you will need to come to an agreement about how the property is to be divided. If the property is in negative equity then you are dividing a debt that you both took on together or you may decide to rent out the property hoping that the value of the property will increase in the future. One of you may decide to stay in the property and pay the other rent.

If you can't agree what to do with your home after you separate then you'll have to go to court. Your lawyer will advise you on the proper proceedings that need to be drafted for your case; if you aren't recognised by law as cohabitants you can't make an application under the 2010 Act so it may be an application to partition the property or divide the beneficial interest of the property.

Sometimes judges will hear applications from couples who have lived together in a 'familial situation' in the family courts. It can be a good option for you to be heard in the family courts if you are a parent with responsibility for children and you're also seeking maintenance. A judge can then get an overall picture of your circumstances as a couple rather than dealing with you as two individuals in a purely commercial transaction.

If you were living with your partner and your name wasn't registered on the property as a joint owner or tenant in common and you aren't recognised by law as a cohabitant then you may have no rights at all. A contribution to the purchase price of the house or mortgage may be recognised by the courts in subsequent proceedings. Your ex may be able to sell the house you live in and get an order to have you moved out. You are putting yourself in a very vulnerable situation when you decide to live in a house without any legal rights. You can be left without a home after spending time living in what you thought of as your 'home', bringing up your children and looking after your partner's house.

A Joint Business or Family Business

If you and your ex are involved in a family business you will have to make decisions in relation to how you will both organise the business or your employment in the business during and after your separation, dissolution, redress application or divorce.

The first thing you need to clarify for yourself is the status of the business. Is it a partnership? Is one of you the sole trader and the other an employee? Is it a limited liability company? Are other family members involved? The status of the business is very important. For example if you work for a large company owned by your ex's family your employment may be protected by employment laws. If you are a shareholder and director of a limited liability company with your ex then you will have continuing duties and obligations under the Companies Acts.

You will have to decide what involvement you want to continue to have in the family business. Do you want to keep working in the company? Do you want to continue to be a director? Would you prefer if your ex bought you out of the business?

The level of conflict between you and your ex will have an influence on your decision. If your separation and divorce have been very acrimonious then it may be impossible for you both to continue to work together. If the company is large and you have an employment contract that you don't wish to terminate then you can keep your employment.

If the business is owned by both of you and one person wishes to buy the other out then you will need to get an accountant to put a value on the business. There are many formulas for calculating the value of a business and an accountant will help you with the calculations and tax implications. A thorough valuation of the business can be very expensive, so if the business isn't doing well it might not be worth paying for a valuation.

The person who decides to keep the business will invariably try to say that it's not doing well so that they can purchase it for the lowest price possible. It's human nature. He or she may even run down or deliberately sabotage the business during negotiations.

It's important to look at your negotiations globally. If your ex is willing to accept or offer a deal that is fair in all the circumstances and the family business is considered in the whole equation then that might be a better way of ensuring a fair deal. For example, rather than forcing your ex to buy your share in the business you might work out a deal where you get generous maintenance. The same will apply to the family or shared home. The person who continues to reside in the family or shared home may receive a smaller maintenance offer.

Savings

Once separation, divorce, dissolution of a civil partnership or redress proceedings by a cohabitant are issued you are obliged to give all the details of your property, income and savings. It's against the law not to disclose the details and you could end up in serious trouble if you lie about your assets. All your savings, whether they are in your sole name, your ex's name or your joint names, are taken into account as part of the assets that are up for division by negotiation or by the courts. The courts will look at the a global picture of what you have and what your ex has and you don't have any automatic right to keep specific savings for yourself.

Pensions

Your private pension is a valuable part of the marital, civil partnership or cohabitation assets and the court can look at pensions and divide the benefits between you and your ex. If one spouse, civil partner or cohabitant has no pension because he or she has been working in the home or working part-time and the other spouse, civil partner or cohabitant has a valuable pension then the court can divide up the benefits. This is known as a pension adjustment order. The court can order that part or all of a specific pension be paid to one spouse, civil partner or cohabitant or that a pension fund in one person's name be put in the other person' name. The court will consider all the financial assets and income of the relationship when making the decision on how to adjust pensions.

There are different types of pensions and there are different types of tax reliefs for different schemes:

- Occupational pensions: Occupational pensions are organised by employers and pay out to their employees on retirement or to their surviving dependants if they die. Employers and employees pay into contributory occupational pension schemes and employers only pay into non-contributory occupational pension schemes.

Most occupational schemes are paid out from a designated fund except for public service pensions, which are funded by the state.

- Defined benefit schemes and defined contribution schemes: A defined benefit scheme is one where the retirement income is based on defined criteria, such as your length of service and pay. You know what your pension will be before you retire by reference to those criteria. A defined contribution scheme is one where the contribution is fixed by agreement but the benefits are decided by the value of the contributions at the time of retirement.

- Personal pension schemes: A personal pension scheme is organised by a self-employed person or an employee who has no occupational pension scheme in their place of work. It pays out to the contributor on retirement or to their surviving dependants if they die.

- Personal Retirement Saving Accounts (PRSA): PRSAs are government-regulated, low-cost, easy-to-access private pension saving accounts. They are designed to give people a flexible way to save for retirement and can be used by employers who do not wish to set up occupational pension schemes. They may also be used to supplement occupational scheme benefits and as a substitute for personal pension schemes.

The Pensions Board is the regulatory body for occupational pensions and it will supervise the operation of the Pensions Act and pension development generally. The Ombudsman for Pensions has the power to investigate and determine your complaints and disputes in relation to your pension.

Holiday Home

A holiday home is an asset like every other asset. Even if it was in your family for centuries it still becomes part of the proceedings. Major difficulties and resentments can arise where a holiday home is in your or your ex's name and is regularly used by other family members. Holiday homes will be treated in the same way as any other asset and can be sold or transferred to one spouse, civil partner or cohabitant or the other or to a dependent family member.

Stocks, Shares and Bonds

You have a legal duty to disclose all your stocks, shares and bonds, and any income from them. They are part of the marital, civil partnership or cohabitation assets and can be divided up as part of the separation, divorce, dissolution or redress proceedings.

Succession Rights

Succession in Ireland is governed by the Succession Act 1965. If your spouse or civil partner dies you have an automatic right to a share in his or her estate. Even if you have lived apart from your spouse or civil partner for a long time you are still entitled to a share of his or her estate if you are still technically married or civil partners. If there is no valid will and no children then you are entitled to the whole of your spouse's or civil partner's estate. If there are children or grandchildren then you are entitled to two-thirds of the estate and the children or grandchildren are entitled to one-third.

If there is a valid will you are entitled to one half of your spouse's estate if there are no children. If there is a valid will and children or grandchildren you are entitled to one-third of your spouse's or civil partner's estate. You should apply for your legal share as soon as possible.

If you decide to separate by signing an agreement together without going to court you can put a clause in your separation agreement renouncing your rights to your spouse's or civil partner's estate voluntarily. When the court grants a decree of separation or dissolution it can extinguish succession rights if either party applies and if it is satisfied that adequate provision exists for the spouse whose rights are being extinguished.

If you get divorced or your civil partnership is dissolved then you are no longer married or in a civil partnership and you no longer have any succession rights. If you are divorced or your civil partnership was dissolved and your ex didn't remarry or enter into a new civil partnership then you can apply for a share in your ex-spouse's estate but you must make the application within six months of the grant of probate or administration.

If you are not married to or in a civil partnership with your partner you are only entitled to a bequest from his or her will.

Personal Possessions

Personal possessions get divided when a relationship end. If one of you moves out of your shared home then usually you will take your own specific personal possessions such as clothes, computers, family heirlooms, pictures, books, music, and perhaps a few items of furniture.

Some couples leave personal possessions in the family home without defining who now owns them, or retain certain things as joint possessions. If you agree to allow your ex to leave his or her bicycle/car/books in the family home for a few years because he or she doesn't have room in the new apartment you are providing a storage facility.

There's no harm in maintaining joint possessions or keeping some things in different locations as long as you are both happy with that arrangement. Be careful because possessions left by your ex in your home can become an excuse to invade your privacy. If the family computer is being used for emails on a daily basis then perhaps you are being too accommodating. A good rule is that as long as the possessions are kept in boxes or don't need to be accessed on a regular basis then it is okay to keep them in the family home.

If there is high conflict post break-up then dividing possessions can become a battleground. You can use your solicitor if you feel it's necessary and try to resolve possession division by exchanging lists and correspondence. If it is very fraught you may need to set up a meeting to negotiate with lawyers or a mediator over who gets what, but this can get expensive.

If you can't agree at all and the possessions are very valuable then you'll have to go to court. If the possessions aren't valuable, you'll probably find that the legal fees you will have to pay to fight over them are prohibitive and that a busy judge won't have the time or the inclination to make pronouncements on who gets the sofa or the cutlery.

If you are on good enough terms then there are a few methods you can use to divide up your joint possessions. First of all you should both take your own personal possessions that are not in dispute and agree that they are not in issue. If you don't want his or her clothes and your ex doesn't want your photos, car or computer then you're halfway there. Then you should both make a list of all the possessions that are in dispute. Agree that these are things that you both would like. Don't be spiteful or dispute possession over something that is definitely of sentimental value to one of you. Once you have a list drawn up of the possessions that are in dispute you can do one of the following:

- Flip a coin. The winner divides the list of disputed possessions into two lists. The loser gets to pick one of the lists.

- Flip a coin. The winner assigns a financial value to each of the items on the list. The loser gets to pick items up to half the value of the total value of the list.

- Get a neutral third party to assign a value to everything and flip a coin. The winner gets to pick the first item. The loser picks the second item and so on until one of you has half the value of all the items.

- Failing agreement, have a garage sale and divide the proceeds or give the disputed items to a charity shop.

Bankruptcy, Mortgages and Debt Management

Bankruptcy

Bankruptcy is a way to settle your debts when you can't pay them. It has far-reaching implications and a very small number of people are declared bankrupt in Ireland each year. In 2010 the courts authorised only 29 bankruptcies. If you can't pay your debts your creditors (people you owe money to) can take you to court and seek to have you judged as bankrupt or you can declare yourself bankrupt. If that happens all the debtor's assets are vested in an official assignee and then shared and distributed between the creditors. The bankrupt is then closely supervised and cannot do certain things (like form or manage a company) for twelve years. The government is looking at ways of changing the laws on bankruptcy so that the effects of an authorised bankruptcy are less severe.

In the United Kingdom there is a process known as an individual voluntary arrangement (IVA), which is a court-supervised legal process that allows individuals to work with insolvency practitioners to reach agreements with their creditors so that they can avoid bankruptcy. Far more people are affected by their day-to-day difficulties in paying their mortgage, utilities and other outgoings than the threat of bankruptcy.

Your Mortgage

If your income is reduced and you are finding it difficult to pay your mortgage you may be able to qualify for a short-term weekly payment from the HSE called a Mortgage Interest Supplement. This only helps you repay the interest on your mortgage and not the capital.

If you have a spare room in your home you can rent out a room to a private tenant. Up to €10,000 of your rental income is exempt from tax and you don't have to register as a landlord.

If you are covered by a mortgage protection policy your mortgage will be repaid if you die or it may cover payments if you lose your job.

The Central Bank of Ireland has a code of conduct on mortgage arrears and it requires lenders to be sympathetic and positive to borrowers who are in mortgage arrears. Repossessing your home should be the last resort. The lender's objective should be to help people meet their mortgage obligations. The lenders must operate a Mortgage Arrears Resolution Process (MARP), which has five steps that should be followed:

1. Communication: The lender must inform you of the status of your account and keep you informed of the potential of legal proceedings, the importance of taking advice and the implications of the sale of your property.

2. Financial information and assessment: The lender must give you a standard financial statement for you to fill out that gives you both an accurate picture of your financial situation and then assess your case on its individual merits.

3. Resolution: The lender must explore all options for alterative repayment such as interest-only arrangements or extending the term of the mortgage. If the lender isn't willing to give you an alternative arrangement it must give you a reason why in writing.

4. Appeals: You can appeal the lender's decision in writing to the Lender's Appeals Board, which will consider it and give you a decision within eight weeks.

5. Repossession proceedings: The lender must not apply to court to repossess your property until every reasonable effort has been made to reach an alternative agreement.

Debt Management

In Ireland we have a court-controlled system that allows people in financial difficulties (debtors) to be taken to court by the people they owe money to (creditors). If you are being taken to court for a debt and you have a good defence you may qualify for legal services from the Legal Aid Board. If you don't have a good defence you won't get legal services. You can pay the debt in full or come to an agreement with your creditor to pay the debt by instalments before the court date. If the court makes a judgment against you the creditor's costs in taking the case are added to your debt.

Once your creditor obtains judgment against you he or she is entitled to apply to use different ways of 'enforcing' or getting the money from you. There are a number of different ways a creditor can enforce the judgment to get his or her money from you, for example, by attachment of your earnings (requiring your employer to take money from your earnings at source to pay your debt), an instalment order, a judgment mortgage on your property (a judgment can be registered as a mortgage against your house for twelve years and if your house is sold it will have to be paid off) or execution against your goods (the sheriff comes to your house and can seize goods to the value of the debt).

Many people are in arrears on their utility bills and are unable to pay for their basic services. The ESB, Bord Gais and other utility companies are working closely with the Money Advice and Budgeting Service (MABS) and other voluntary agencies to help their customers who are in difficulties. Some customers are installing pay-as-you-go metering systems in their houses for their utilities and many are entering into special payment arrangements or signing up with An Post's Household Budget Scheme to avoid disconnection. Other customers are returning to using solid fuel such as coal and briquettes to heat their homes when they can afford to.

Always engage with your debtors and take advice from MABS. It provides an excellent service for people who are in financial difficulties and will give solid practical and legal advice on how to manage your mortgage arrears and debts for free.

The Irish government is looking at different ways of helping people who can't pay the arrears on their mortgages, which are in negative equity, and can't pay their debts. In the future there may be laws introduced regulating debt settlement arrangements, personal insolvency arrangements, debt relief or debt forgiveness. These laws would ease the burden on people who can't afford to pay their mortgages or debts and allow them to effectively wipe the slate clean on more favourable terms than are possible at present.

Budgeting

Budgeting is putting down on paper where your money comes from, how much you have and where it's going.

Making a budget is quite difficult because spending varies so much over different periods of time. Purchasing big items like houses and cars can completely ruin or distort your budget. Your attitude to money will affect your budget hugely. As more money comes in you may feel an overwhelming need to spend it. If you're a saver you won't.

Unless you have a fixed income and fixed outgoings it's hard to put together an accurate budget that will work in the long term. You will need to keep changing and updating it as your circumstances change.

Drawing Up a Budget

Gather together all the pieces of paper in your house that relate to your finances. Keep all your receipts and look at all your utility bills, mortgage payments, rent, credit card payments, clothing expenses, supermarket receipts, entertainment receipts, car loans, mobile phone bills, school or grind fees, medical insurance, GP bills, fuel bills, etc. Put them in a pile. Go through them, go online and call up service providers for additional information. Small amounts of money that you spend on a daily basis on parking, coffee, sandwiches, newspapers and other items can build up as well. It's worth taking the time to write down these outgoings on a notebook for a month or two. The results may surprise you. Try to average out your spending over two years on everything. That will give you an idea of your outgoings each month.

Get an accurate record of all your sources of income. If you have a monthly take home pay cheque then that's it. Look at other sources of income such as government benefits. If you're self-employed it's more difficult, especially if your income is falling. Go over your accounts for a few years and try to get an idea of the average amount of your income over time.

Divide up your spending into necessities/needs and luxuries/wants. Your necessities are the roof over your head, food, electricity and heating. Your luxuries might be eating out or your gym membership. Work out what you can afford to spend each month and try to minimise or spend less on what you can't afford. Keep a record of how you're doing and you will notice where your weaknesses are. It will take time for budgeting to have any effect on your spending but having an accurate picture of where the money is going will help you correct overspending and prioritise your spending.

The aim of analysing your spending is to eventually have control over how much you spend. If you can designate a certain amount of money towards running your household each week or month and stick to that figure then you are successfully budgeting your finances.

Living on Less

There's nothing harder than trying to live on less money than you are used to. Relationship break-ups generally lead to less income for both of you. If you have a budget that you can't keep to then you need to live on less. The most important things are food, shelter and clothing. After that everything else is a plus.

Food is a big expense that can get out of control if you buy without planning. Start by deciding what you are going to eat each week. Make out a menu plan and stick to it. Impulse buying, takeaways and eating in restaurants will mess up your budget.

If you can't cook you or someone in your household must learn to do so. Invest in a freezer so you can buy meat and other items that are on sale. Each item of food should have a day on which it is to be eaten. If you end up with leftovers they should be used for the next day's meal or for soup. A huge amount of food is thrown away uneaten and proper planning will stop you from being in a situation where this happens.

The cost of buying clothing for you and your children can be easily reduced if you have overspent in the past. Chain stores sell low-price clothing and second-hand shops shouldn't be avoided as they can have amazingly inexpensive high quality clothing. If your children require school uniforms ask your school if there is a sale of second-hand clothing.

Housing is a huge cost and in Ireland we are historically drawn towards home ownership. It's nice to own your own home but it's not a must. The advantage of renting is that you can always reduce your overhead by renting a less expensive property if necessary.

Other ways of cutting your costs are by doing a lot of research before you spend money on large items such as your house or health insurance, your car and holidays. Ensuring good energy efficiency by using insulation, proper appliances and proper conservation practices will save you money on your energy bills. House swapping and volunteering to work abroad will make travelling less expensive and growing your own food on an allotment will reduce your grocery bills. Take advantage of free events, libraries and second-hand bookshops and socialise with people who are happy to come over and share a meal and a bottle of wine rather than go to expensive restaurants.

6

Other Issues

Domestic violence – Child abuse – False accusations – Parental child abduction – Lesbian, gay, bisexual and transgender issues – Annulment of your marriage or civil partnership

Domestic Violence

There are differences of opinion in academic and political circles and the media about the incidence of domestic violence against men and women and what the definition of domestic violence is, so this section refers to violence against men and women although some of the organisations and history relate to one sex.

Domestic violence includes physical and severe emotional abuse. In 1997 the *Report of the Irish Government Task Force on Domestic Violence* defined it as: 'the use of physical or emotional force or threat of physical force, including sexual violence, in close adult relationships. This includes violence perpetrated by spouse, partner, son, daughter or any other person who is a close blood relation of the victim.'

Extreme emotional cruelty towards a victim includes behaviours such as bullying or humiliating your victim, forcing your victim to have sex, isolating them from their friends and family, denying them access to money, threatening them, or damaging or destroying their personal property.

Irish people owe a huge debt of gratitude to the many different organisations and people who campaigned for the 1976 Family Law Act, which introduced legislation on domestic violence to Ireland. It allowed a spouse to seek a barring order against another spouse where their or their children's welfare or safety was at risk. The legislation was improved in 1981 with the introduction of protection orders. Before this legislation was introduced a spouse who was being abused faced homelessness if he or she didn't want to live with his or her abusive spouse.

In the 1970s it was assumed that a husband had a right to have sex with his wife and the concept of marital rape didn't exist. Men who committed adultery with a married woman could be sued for 'criminal conversation' and be obliged to pay compensation to the woman's husband for having sex with his wife. Women were considered by law to be objects or 'chattels'.

This situation changed because of campaigning by many organisations, including Women's Aid and the Council for the Status of Women, for the introduction of legislation against marital rape and changes to the law on rape, violence against women and domestic violence. New legislation was introduced to broaden the law on rape in 1981 and marital rape became an offence in 1990.

The Domestic Violence Act was introduced into law in 1996 and it again improved the existing legislation. It allowed the courts to intervene to protect people living in domestic arrangements against danger or threats of danger to their safety or welfare. It allowed the health authorities to apply for barring orders on behalf of victims, and victims to apply for interim barring orders, protection orders and safety orders, which are discussed below.

Domestic violence starts with individual behaviour. The perpetrator may have an alcohol abuse problem, may suffer from mental illness or a personality disorder or there may be no apparent reason. The relationships in households where domestic violence occurs may also be dysfunctional due to low education, poverty, bad parenting or an unhappy marriage.

If domestic violence is a feature of your life, you need to eliminate it before you are severely physically or emotionally injured or killed. You can't negotiate your way out of a situation where you are being abused. The best you can do for yourself is to get advice on how to protect yourself from your abuser. There are different organisations that provide support and legal advice if you are suffering from abuse, such as the Rape Crisis Centre (a support service for all victims of rape), Women's Aid (a support service for women and their children) and AMEN (a support service for men and their children). More information about these organisations and other useful organisations are in the resources section at the back of this book.

Cosc is the National Office for the Prevention of Sexual and Gender-Based Violence and its aim is to deliver a well-coordinated response to domestic violence by working with various groups and government agencies. It facilitates action for the prevention of these crimes, the protection of victims and the provision of services for those affected.

If you are a victim of domestic violence you can seek to have the perpetrator removed from your home or you can leave yourself. If you are afraid for your safety or the safety of your children you ought to seek help from the Gardaí or go into hiding. If you can't find any accommodation you can apply for a place in a women's refuge.

There are about thirteen women's refuges in Ireland and most of them are run by voluntary groups. They all have more women seeking places than they can accommodate. Unfortunately there are no refuges for men who are experiencing domestic violence in Ireland.

According to the Health Service Executive, social workers should not immediately encourage individuals to leave an abusive relationship in case it provokes a 'catastrophic event'. Women and men have to decide themselves when is the best time to leave a relationship or the family home and should do so in a way that is protective of themselves and their children.

What to Do

If you think it is an appropriate course of action you can seek to have the perpetrator of domestic violence removed from your home by court order or you can ask the court to make an order to stop that person from using or threatening to use violence against you without seeking to have them removed from your home. Taking legal action to exclude a person from their home is an extremely serious course of action. Be sure that you have thought carefully about it and taken good advice.

There are a number of different types of orders you can seek so it can be a bit confusing. The four types of orders you can apply for if you are suffering from domestic violence are:

- A safety order: A safety order doesn't remove the perpetrator from your home. It is an order that prohibits a person from using or threatening to use violence against you or your children. That person doesn't have to live with you and if he or she doesn't live in your home they can't watch or be near your home. It can be granted for up to five years.

- A protection order: A protection order is a temporary safety order. The court will make this order until the full hearing of an application for a barring or safety order. It can be made without notice and its effect is similar to a safety order.

- A barring order: A barring order is an order that requires a person to leave your house and stay away from you for a specific time period. The maximum is three years.

- An interim barring order: You can also apply for an interim barring order without notice to the perpetrator which will bar the perpetrator from your home for eight days until a full hearing of the barring order application. There must be an immediate risk of significant harm. The court may require you to swear an affidavit setting out the grounds for your application.

If you want to remove a perpetrator of domestic violence from your home or have an order in place prohibiting them from being violent towards you or your children then you will have to start by going to your local District Court office and fill out a form with the help of a District Court clerk. You will get a date for a hearing and if you are really concerned you can ask the court for an interim order immediately to last until the full hearing.

The District Court can make a safety order for five years and a barring order for three years. You can go back to court to renew the orders after the period has expired.

At interim or full hearings you ought to bring relevant evidence of domestic violence to the court. It may be your own oral evidence, the evidence of a witness, a doctor's evidence, or medical or other reports. The court will have to be satisfied that your safety and welfare are at risk. For an interim barring order to be granted the court must be satisfied that you are at immediate risk of significant harm. In some cases the perpetrator of the domestic violence will consent to an order being made. In other cases both parties may have orders made against them, for example mutual protection orders.

It's a serious step to exclude someone from their home for an interim period of eight days when they haven't been given a chance to have their say. Interim orders are usually made *ex parte* (one side gives evidence only), and doing so with falsified evidence is an offence.

You ought to notify your local Garda station if you have an order in place to protect you. You can bring along a copy of the order and give it into a Garda station yourself. The court will also forward a copy of the order to your local Garda station the next day. If there is a breach of the order you should call the station and inform the Gardaí of the breach. The person who breaches the order is guilty of a criminal offence and can be arrested and prosecuted without a warrant.

Who Can You Get an Order Against?

You are entitled to apply for different domestic violence orders depending on your relationship to the perpetrator. You must check before you make an application for an order whether you are entitled to that specific order against that specific person. The following is a list of some of the people against whom particular orders may be sought:

- Your spouse: It does not matter how long you are living together or who owns your house; you can apply for a barring, interim barring, protection or safety order against your spouse.

- Your civil partner: It does not matter how long you are living together or who owns your house; you can apply for a barring, interim barring, protection or safety order against your civil partner.

- Your cohabitant: You are defined as a cohabitant if you are not married but have been living together for a period of six months in the past year. You must have been living together for six months during a nine-month period. You will not get a barring order if your cohabitant owns the place where you live together or has greater ownership rights than you, otherwise you can apply for a barring, interim barring, protection or safety order against your cohabitant.

- Your children: You can apply for an order against your adult child if he or she is over eighteen and not dependent on you. You can apply for a barring, interim barring, protection or safety order against your adult children.

- A person you are living with in a non-contractual relationship, such as a relative: You can apply for protection and safety orders against people with whom you are living in a non-contractual domestic arrangement.

If the Health Service Executive is of the opinion that the safety or welfare of a child is in danger it may seek a barring order on behalf of a child against an adult living in their home.

If domestic violence laws do not protect you and you are in fear of violence you ought to go to the Gardaí and report the perpetrator. You can always report an incident of domestic violence to the Gardaí whether or not you have an order in place.

Child Abuse

What Is Abuse?

Many children in Ireland suffer physical, emotional and sexual abuse and neglect. If you suspect that your partner or another adult or child is neglecting or abusing a child then you ought to seek help as soon as possible. Different organisations have different guidelines and codes of conduct for people who work with or come into contact with children and suspect abuse. There is also immunity from civil liability to any person who 'reasonably and in good faith' reports child abuse to the HSE or the Gardaí.

- *Emotional abuse* occurs where a parent is emotionally unavailable to or negative towards a child, is overly harsh, ignores a child, is unaffectionate, exposes a child to violence or is unrealistic or inappropriate in their attitude towards their child.

- *Physical abuse* is harm or injury to a child, shaking, allowing a child to be exposed to a risky situation, suffocation, poisoning or Münchausen syndrome by proxy (a condition where a parent or adult fabricates a story of illness about a child or causes signs of illness).

- *Sexual abuse* includes things such as touching or molesting a child for the purpose of arousal, performing a sexual act with a child or performing a sexual act in front of a child, involving a child in masturbation, or sexually exploiting a child by involving them in modelling or posing in a sexual manner, or encouraging children in consensual sexual acts when they are aged under 17.

- *Neglect* is another form of abuse and it occurs when a child is harmed because they are deprived of things such as food, clothes, warmth, hygiene, intellectual stimulation, supervision, safety, attachment to and affection from adults, and medical care.

Certain things are obvious indicators that there are serious problems but other things are subtle so you should always be mindful of the signs of abuse.

What Are the Signs to Watch Out For?

Signs of abuse can be physical or manifest themselves in behaviour. Look at the behaviour of the child, his or her interactions with others and the person you suspect to be the abuser. If the child makes a direct or indirect statement to you that they are being hurt or abused in any way you ought to believe the child. Suicide attempts, running away from home, sexually transmitted diseases, pregnancy, unexplained physical injuries, abnormal development, and abnormal sexual play or behaviour are all possible indicators of abuse.

What Should You Do?

If you suspect something is amiss go and seek help from the police. You can also seek additional help from the health services, the hospital, a social worker or a doctor. Many organisations have guidelines and codes of conduct which set out the duty of care its members or employees have in relation to reporting their concerns or suspicions of child abuse.

Guidelines in Ireland

Children First – National Guidelines for the Protection and Welfare of Children was published in 1999. The guidelines are aimed at a wide audience of people who have contact with children or provide services for children, for example teachers, childcare workers, heathcare workers, volunteers and youth workers. It emphasises the needs of children and gives guidelines that any person who is in contact with children and suspects that a child is abused or at risk of abuse should make a report to the HSE or Gardaí without delay.

An Ombudsman for Children was appointed in 2003 to deal with complaints by and on behalf of children and to promote the rights and welfare of young people.

In a new departure in 2011 the Fine Gael–Labour government appointed a Minister for Children and Youth Affairs, giving children a full minister and government department of their own rather than providing for them as part of the Department of Health.

At present there is no law requiring the mandatory reporting of child sexual abuse allegations but legislation is in train and it will apply to voluntary and statutory organisations and faith-based groups.

False Accusations

People can and do make false accusations of domestic violence and sexual abuse, especially when conflict is high during break-ups and family law proceedings. If your ex is malicious or angry, wants to punish you, or feels frustrated or powerless he or she might resort to making false allegations. This will put you in an extremely difficult position. You will have to decide whether to fight to refute the false allegations or you can try to stop your ex from going down that route by agreeing to a separation or a divorce if you think that is a better course of action. Before you make a decision on what to do you should seek legal advice.

Be careful to avoid conduct that could be misconstrued, especially if you are in a new relationship with someone who has contact with your children. Don't let new partners engage in any verbal or physical conduct that might be considered inappropriate. The family law courts operate differently to the criminal courts, the rules of evidence are less stringent and the best interests of the child are seen as paramount so it can be difficult to prove that you weren't violent or abusive in the context of family law proceedings if a false allegation is made.

If you have been unfairly barred from your house you can appeal the order: prepare your evidence very carefully and hire a really good solicitor or barrister to give you the best representation possible so you have a good chance of having the barring order overturned. If your ex has barred you unfairly it probably signifies that the relationship is over so you ought to issue judicial separation or divorce proceedings as soon as you can so that parental responsibilities, property and income issues can be resolved.

If you have been falsely accused of abuse or violence you must try to maintain a positive relationship with your children. If you are seeing them under supervised access or very occasionally don't get angry. Try to keep calm and concentrate on preparing your case for a full appeal of the unfair order. Sometimes the court will order a child protection enquiry if the judge or the HSE is concerned.

If your situation is being investigated and you have to be interviewed by a social worker, psychiatrist, psychologist, doctor or Garda make sure you turn up, cooperate and tell the truth. Once any kind of investigation or enquiry into the welfare of your children or your behaviour is in train you should cooperate honestly and fully. If you feel that the investigations or enquiries are being conducted unfairly you ought to ask your solicitor for advice on what to do.

If you are preparing to refute false allegations of violence or abuse try not to be consumed by anger. You will need to keep a clear head so that you can get all the evidence and support that you need. Take statements or ask your solicitor to take statements from family, friends, teachers, doctors and other professionals who know your family. If your ex fabricated evidence or documents or had a witness in court who was telling lies make sure you have a good barrister and solicitor at the time of your appeal who can help you to prove that the evidence was fabricated and thoroughly cross-examine the witness who was lying.

If you suspect that a false allegation is about to be made against you make sure you keep very good records of where you are and what happens around that time; try to have an independent witness around if possible.

If you have to go to court to appeal an unjust order make sure you prepare your evidence well, keep a cool head and put your time and energy into the case and do not violate any order made against you. Don't get angry and aggressive as this will work against you, and never admit to anything that isn't true even if it seems like the easiest thing to do.

Parental Child Abduction

If you have a right of custody in relation to your child, and your child is under 16 and habitually resident in Ireland, then that child cannot be removed from Ireland by your co-parent without your permission. If your co-parent does take your child to another country and that country is a signatory of the Hague Convention then you have some protection under the Hague Convention on the Civil Aspects of International Child Abduction.

The Hague Convention has been signed by over 80 countries. It was set up so that children who have been removed from one country to another country that is also a signatory can be returned as soon as possible. It's there to ensure that custody issues between parents are decided in the country where the child habitually resides.

Your child won't be returned if the courts in the contracting country decide that your child would be at grave risk of harm in Ireland or if the child objects to being returned to Ireland and is old and mature enough to have his or her views taken into account. The Department of Justice is the central authority that deals with applications to have your child returned under the Hague Convention.

Many countries, including all European countries and the United States, are signatories. It's not the first thing people think about but if you are in a relationship with a foreign national you might want to check if his or her country of origin is a signatory. If you have a child with someone whose country is not a signatory to the Convention and your child is ever abducted by them back to their country of origin you will face huge difficulties trying to get your child back to Ireland because you will probably have to apply for the return of your child through the local legal system. The local legal system may not recognise parents' rights or children's rights in the same way as they are recognised in Ireland.

The Luxembourg Convention on Recognition and Enforcement of Decisions Concerning Custody of Children and on Restoration of Custody of Children is designed to ensure that custody and access orders are enforced in contracting countries.

If you break up and your co-parent wants to take your child to live in another country for work reasons or because they've started a relationship with someone who lives in another country this can cause serious difficulties. If you agree that your child can live abroad then you will have to work out access to take account of your locations.

If you live in Ireland and your child lives in London then it will be inconvenient and expensive but possible to work out a schedule. If your child is going to the US, for example, then it's much more difficult. As a parent you are in a long-term committed relationship with your child and you must take their needs into account. Many Irish people work in the UK for economic reasons and commute back home regularly to see their children.

If your co-parent wants to move further away and you don't agree to the move then the matter will end up in court and a judge will make the decision for you both. The judge will decide what is best for the child considering all the circumstances.

As Ireland has seen an influx of immigrants and many Irish people work and travel abroad it is not surprising that there's been a huge increase in inter-country marriages between Irish nationals and nationals from other countries. If you're happily married and you like visiting your in-laws in France, the United Kingdom, Egypt, India or the United States then that's fine. It will only become a problem if you break up and your ex wants to move back home with your child.

It's important to always put your children first and they ought to reside where they are happiest. In general it is unfair to ask a child to leave the security of their home, family, friends, schools and extended family if you want to leave Ireland for selfish reasons. Parents need to balance their children's needs with their own needs. If all your friends and family are in your native country you may feel you need to move back home for support if your relationship has broken down. It's a very difficult decision.

Sometimes your family will have to move with you if your job takes you abroad or you have to emigrate for economic reasons. Most children don't like change but they can and do adapt.

The big problem arises when your ex decides that he or she is going to take your child to another country without your permission. There is a growing problem in Ireland of this type of abduction, especially to countries that don't recognise the Hague Convention.

The Irish Centre for Parentally Abducted Children

The Irish Centre for Parentally Abducted Children (ICPAC) sets out guidelines for the prevention of child abduction that are extremely useful if you fear that your co-parent is going to abduct your child. You should always seek help and legal advice if such a situation arises. If you fear an imminent abduction contact your solicitor, the Gardaí, the Department of Justice and the ICPAC as soon as you can and seek help and information from them.

If you fear abduction keep your child's passport safe, although having your child's passport will not stop your child being abducted. If your child's passport is missing or stolen report the matter to the Gardaí. If your co-parent won't give you your child's passport and you're worried about abduction seek legal advice. If there's a court order that obliges you or your co-parent to surrender your child's passport the Passport Office should be notified and presented with a copy of the order so that another passport can't be issued. If you think your child has another nationality or passport check with the embassy or consulate of that other country.

The ICPAC gives practical advice in its *Guidelines for the Prevention of Abduction* booklet. In it, it suggests that you ought to fill out a very comprehensive description form for all your children who you think are at risk of abduction and of the potential abductor. It also suggests that for each child you complete a fingerprint form, take colour photographs and DNA samples, and make copies of birth certificates and court orders. It gives instructions on how to take hair samples. You should also try to get photographs of the potential abductor. Write the name of the person, the date of birth of the person and the date the photograph was taken on the back of all the photographs. Fill out a details form for yourself and enclose marriage certificates and court orders relating to your marriage or separation. It says that you ought to make up sets of the above documents and give them to the Gardaí and your solicitor.

If you think your child is about to be abducted tell your local Gardaí and give them all the documents. If the Gardaí think the threat of abduction is real and imminent they will issue an 'All Ports Alert'. This is only a notification procedure and won't necessarily prevent your child from being abducted but it will alert the Gardaí and officials at points of entry and exit to the country such as airports, ports and borders. The Gardaí have the power to detain a child whom they reasonably suspect is about to be removed in breach of a court order regarding custody or access.

If your child has been abducted to another country the Department of Foreign Affairs can provide you with some information and assistance in relation to lawyers in the country your child has been abducted to.

Ask the Registrar of Births if anyone has made an application for your child's birth certificate. If you become aware that it has been issued then you ought to notify the Gardaí of this and of the imminent danger of your child being abducted.

Tell people who have contact with your children of your fears, e.g. teachers, doctors, social workers, childminders, parents of their friends and youth club leaders.

Lesbian, Gay, Bisexual and Transgender Issues

Lesbian, gay, bisexual and transgender people (LGBT) have access to nearly all of the same services as heterosexual people when they experience relationship breakdown. LGBT.ie is a useful website that has a comprehensive list of helplines and support available: they are the same organisations used by heterosexual people and other organisations specifically set up for LGBT people. The Family Support Agency will offer counselling and the Family Mediation Service will offer mediation to LGBT people in the event of relationship breakdown and other free services are equally accessible. Remedies for victims of domestic violence are available for LGBT people who are cohabiting or who have registered civil partnerships.

At present sex changes are not legally recognised in Ireland so transgender people who wish to have their birth certificates changed to legally reflect the change in their gender cannot do so. This means that transgender people cannot get married in civil ceremonies if they have changed their gender. They can enter a civil partnership with someone of the same sex that is stated on their birth certificate.

The Gender Recognition Advisory Group set up by the government presented a report in 2011 advising recommendations for a scheme to allow transgender people to apply for legal recognition of their gender change on their birth certificates. The group recommended that applicants fulfil the medical criteria of gender identity disorder diagnosis or present evidence of gender reassignment surgery and suggested that an applicant should be single, which would mean that they might have to choose between having their gender legally recognised and remaining in their marriage or civil partnership. The Transgender Equality Network says these recommendations are stigmatising and outdated.

The Civil Partnership and Certain Rights and Obligations of Cohabitants Act 2010 allows same sex couples to register their relationships as civil partnerships with a registrar. The rights and obligations of same sex couples in registered civil partnerships are similar to but less than the rights and obligations of heterosexual married couples. Civil partnerships aren't treated as being as important as the institution of marriage. For example, it is easier to end a civil partnership (you need to be living apart for two of the previous three years), you can't apply for a judicial separation, you may be required at a criminal trial to give evidence against your civil partner (spouses aren't), you have to be eighteen to register a civil partnership (you can be younger to marry), and there is no requirement to be given information about mediation by your solicitor if you are considering the dissolution of your civil partnership.

Same sex partners in registered civil partnerships are treated similarly but not equally in areas such as taxation, family law, maintenance, emigration, housing, court procedures, inheritance, freedom of information and other miscellaneous areas.

Marriage Equality have published a report called *Missing Pieces*, available online from marriagequality.ie, which compares the rights and responsibilities gained from civil partnership with the rights and responsibilities gained through civil marriage in Ireland. The report found 169 differences in the treatment of civil partners in the areas outlined above which apply to married couples but not civil partners.

The report states that civil partnership is unequal to marriage in many different ways and the law doesn't recognise a same sex couple with children as a family in the same way as children brought up within a marriage. Same sex couples have a serious difficulty if they are bringing up children together as a couple or as civil partners because the non-adoptive or non-biological partner can be fulfilling the role of parent to the child without having any legally defined role as a parent or guardian. A same sex couple can apply to foster as there is a shortage of foster parents.

The 'family home' for married couples is treated different to the 'shared home' for civil partners under the 2010 Act. Dependent children living with married couples in the 'family home' are defined as 'non-biological children', which is a broad category. The law is protective of children living with step-parents. Children living with same sex parents aren't given the same protection of their home under the 2010 Act.

Same sex couples aren't allowed to adopt children together whether they are in a civil partnership or not. Single LGBT individuals may apply to adopt as single adoptive parents.

If a couple in a same sex relationship hits difficulties then they can use the same services as everyone else. Most counselling services cater for same sex couples and solicitors and barristers are there to help in the event of disagreements over property and finances. The issues are dealt with differently by law depending on whether you are in a long-term relationship, cohabiting or civil partners.

Annulment of your Marriage or Civil Partnership

If you think your marriage or civil partnership was invalid or never existed legally you can apply to court for an order of annulment. The effect of this order is that in the eyes of the law your marriage or civil partnership never happened so the rights and responsibilities that flowed from the status of being married or in a civil partnership are also extinguished.

If you or your ex gets an order for nullity it has very serious and far-reaching consequences for you both. As far as the law is concerned you were never married or your civil partnership was never registered (because, for example, certain formalities weren't followed or you didn't have the capacity to enter into a contract with each other) – your children aren't the children of the marriage and a whole range of legal protections and remedies are no longer applicable to either of you. There is no longer any protection for the family home under the Family Home Protection Act, or the 'shared home' under the 2010 Act, you are not entitled to apply for maintenance as a spouse or a civil partner and all the remedies available under the Family Law, Judicial Separation, Divorce and Civil Partnership Acts are no longer available to you.

If your ex commences proceedings to annul your marriage or civil partnership and you want to defend the application then you will definitely need a good lawyer. The proceedings can be lengthy and expensive, and if he or she succeeds the repercussions are enormous.

Civil and Ecclesiastical Nullity

Lots of people get confused between civil and ecclesiastical nullities. There are two types of marriages: civil (recognised by the state) and ecclesiastical (recognised by the Catholic Church and other religions). When couples get married in Catholic or other religious ceremonies they also sign a register; this is the part of the marriage that gives it legal effect or recognition by the state. The religious ceremony is separate.

If you get a civil annulment you can get married afterwards by civil ceremony (but not in a religious ceremony if you were previously married in a religious ceremony). If you apply for an annulment through the ecclesiastical courts and you are granted an ecclesiastical annulment you can marry again in a church (but not in a civil ceremony unless you are divorced or have a civil annulment). Some people look for civil annulments only because they want to assert their legal rights; others look for ecclesiastical annulments for religious reasons. Sometimes people make applications for both but they must go through separate procedures for both.

The Catholic Church has its own ecclesiastical courts and grounds for annulment that are not dealt with here. Other religions have other rules for the dissolution or annulment of marriages. Different religions accept different reasons as grounds for annulment and they differ from the grounds for a civil annulment.

If you wish to seek a dissolution or annulment of your marriage by your church, mosque, synagogue or other place of worship then you should talk to your local priest or religious leader who will provide you with information on how to apply and the names of lawyers who specialise in religious laws and applications to religious courts.

There are five grounds for a civil annulment of marriages and three for civil partnerships.

Grounds for annulment of both marriages and civil partnerships:

- You were not capable of marrying each other or registering a civil partnership. This is called lack of capacity. It may be because you were of the same sex (for marriage), under age and had no permission from the court to marry, already married or in a civil partnership, or within forbidden degrees of blood relationship (brother and sister, for example).

- You did not properly observe the formalities of a marriage or civil partnership. For example you didn't sign the Register or give proper notice to the Register of Marriages or Civil Partnerships.

- There was an absence of consent. If one of you didn't give full, free and informed consent then the marriage or civil partnership isn't valid. For example, if you were threatened, pressurised or suffering from a mental illness and for that reason you couldn't give your consent.

Grounds for annulment of a marriage only:

- You could not consummate the marriage. If you can't have sex with the person you're married to because of physical or psychological impotence then the marriage can be annulled.

- If you are unable to enter into and sustain a normal marital relationship. For example if you are mentally ill to such an extent that you have no capacity to be married or you are homosexual then the marriage can be annulled.

If you want to bring an application to annul your marriage or civil partnership for any of the above reasons you must prove to the court that your marriage or civil partnership was not valid. Annulment applications are usually handled by lawyers who are experts in the area of family law. Since the introduction of divorce into Ireland there have been less nullity applications.

Judges are aware that some applicants will try to use the law of nullity as a way to avoid the legal and financial responsibilities that go with marriage and civil partnership. Sometimes judges will enquire into the financial arrangements that the couple have established and are concerned to make sure that the law of nullity isn't used by either party to penalise the other, especially where the relationship has been a long one and there are children from the relationship.

7

Your New Life

*Your new circle – Behaving well – New partners and step-parenting –
New friends and dating*

Your New Circle

You've put lots of time, energy and effort into making your break-up as amicable as you possibly can. Your children are in a routine, you have somewhere to live, life is less turbulent and you've settled your issues. You've gone to a mediator, negotiated your case, fought through the courts and you now have a copy of your separation agreement, court order or divorce decree. You've come out the other side of your break-up, not bitter but slightly battered and wiser.

You have a new identity that includes your break-up and its effect on you. You have children, an experience of high conflict or a new financial situation that are part of you and your history.

Irish people have a strong sense of community; they love to gossip and chat and people often know all about you before you've met them. It's nice to live in a country where people take an interest in each other but if you've been through a break-up Irish cities, towns and villages can feel very small. You may find yourself answering extremely personal questions or explaining your situation defensively to new acquaintances.

Don't ever be pressurised into answering personal questions if you don't feel like it. If you are asked about your ex or your new relationship after your break-up keep your answers brief and change the subject. If the question is really personal and you find it insulting or rude just say to the person who asked it, 'That's a personal/private matter and I don't want to discuss it.' Then you should change the subject.

If you move on and forge new relationships there will be added complications in your life. Your children will be introduced to your new partner. Your ex will introduce your children to his or her new partner. You will meet your partner's new children and stepchildren, your old friends who still like your ex will meet his or her new partner. Your circle will be bigger; there will be new relationships and potential for conflict to enter your life again.

You can't exclude the new people who enter your circle. If your ex meets a new partner then that person will possibly meet and form relationships with your children, family and friends. If you are rude to, ignore or avoid the new people in your circle you will create conflict and you and your children will suffer. It is better to accept that these new people are now part of your life and decide how to incorporate them into your life. You don't have to be best friends. Your aim is to be able to maintain a cordial, polite, non-confrontational relationship with everyone.

Be careful to keep your old circle intact. If you meet someone new it's natural to be excited and happy and want to spend all your time together. It's equally important to stay in contact with your old friends and not to neglect your family. Keep a cool head. You still have obligations to your own circle and if things don't work out with your new relationship you will want the support of your friends. Equally, if things are going well with your new partner there's no rush. Hopefully you'll end up in a stable permanent relationship with your new partner, so there's no need to neglect your life for theirs.

If you behave well after separation and divorce and approach the new people in your circle in a genuinely open and welcoming way then you will find your own life to be a lot richer and fulfilling. It's not always easy if the new person in your circle is unfriendly or aggressive towards you. You can only control your own behaviour so your responsibility is to behave well and try to make things as smooth and conflict-free as possible for your children. If you're lonely and want to get out, make new friends and socialise there are some suggestions on how to meet new people at the end of this chapter.

Behaving Well

Who are these new people in your life? What relationships should you have with them? How do you minimise conflict with your ex? Your new partner is going to be delightful and important to you, but your ex's new partner may well be a thorn in your side. Don't start off on the wrong foot. It's important to behave well because if you don't your family and friends will suffer. You have the power to create a ripple of conflict that can polarise people and create huge difficulties for everyone in your circle.

If you don't have children then you probably won't have to interact very much with your ex. If you still live in the same village or town, or socialise or work in the same circles, then it is important to minimise conflict because you will be meeting each other socially. If you do have children you will have to put your issues aside, put your children first and make an enormous effort to behave well. It's not fair to subject your children to a second wave of conflict because new people are coming into their lives after the break-up.

If you meet a new partner and are planning to introduce them to your children it might be a good idea to discuss it with your co-parent first. If your co-parent hears that you've met someone new and introduced them to your children without you mentioning it to him or her in advance it can be a source of conflict. It's not a good idea to introduce your children to everyone you're dating; it can be upsetting and confusing for them if they see you with lots of new people over a short period of time.

If you think you're going to have a long-term relationship with your new partner then it is appropriate to introduce them to your children. Make sure that your children meet your new partner on a comfortable, stress-free occasion. If he or she drops into the house for a short period, meets your children in their own environment and then leaves your children will feel a lot less stressed and more secure than they would if they met him or her for the first time on a family holiday. If your children are older you can ask them where and when they would like to be introduced to your new partner.

Minimising Conflict with your Ex post Break-Up

How can you minimise conflict in your regular interactions with your ex? If he or she is continually unreliable in relation to pick up times, paying maintenance or other responsibilities how do you express your dissatisfaction? If there are new people in the equation you don't approve of how do you deal with them?

If your ex is driving you crazy because of bad behaviour then you will have to express that to him or her in a rational and controlled manner. There is no point in screaming abuse or giving out in front of your children. Tell your ex you need to talk about your arrangements and try to communicate your problems as calmly and tactfully as possible.

When you are discussing post break-up issues with your ex you must let go of the past. Your relationship is over so don't bring your disappointments and past hurts into the discussion. You have moved on and looking back is negative. Give your ex the benefit of the doubt and try to treat him or her politely and calmly.

Try to discuss the problems that have arisen. Try to mutualise the problems so that they are issues that are of interest to you both. If there are issues that affect your children make it clear that you both have a joint concern for their well-being. Don't make your discussions personal. Try to identify the problem in a non-toxic, non-personal manner. Tell your ex that the problem is 'timekeeping' or 'financial' rather than 'your lateness' or 'your failure to pay maintenance'.

Explain the problem and how it makes you feel. Then explain the effect that the problem and your feelings have on you and your children:

'The problem is timekeeping. The children are continually late for school when you are dropping them off on Mondays. When you are late they get in trouble which is a problem for them and for us as parents. It affects their reputation in school, it affects our reputation as parents and it is causing me difficulties with their teachers. I feel as if you aren't concerned about their well-being and education. This makes me very frustrated and angry.'

Listen actively to the response from your ex and you might want to reframe it in a non-toxic manner if necessary. If he or she says:

'It's not my fault, they're really slow at getting ready, I have to shout at them and they still take their time. They won't get out of bed when I tell them and they take ages to get dressed and they complain that they're tired.'

Listen actively by repeating what your ex is saying:

'So you're saying that it's not your fault, they're really slow at getting ready and it takes them ages and they're tired?'

Your ex might indicate if that is the situation:

'Yes, they're so slow, tired and totally unprepared.'

Try to reframe the problem in a non-toxic manner and suggest some problem-solving solutions:

'The problem seems to be that they're tired and not prepared in the morning. Are they staying up very late on Sunday? Do they have their books and uniforms ready the night before?'

Your ex might acknowledge if this is helpful:

'Yes they won't go to bed and everything is totally disorganised in the morning. It's driving me crazy.'

You might suggest a solution that involves you both taking action:

'Why don't we both talk to the children about bedtime and preparation for school? If you tell them that they have to prepare themselves for school on Sunday afternoon and go to bed earlier then it might be easier to get them into school on time on Monday.'

If you can build a working relationship and successfully communicate and negotiate with your ex around small issues you have a better chance of cooperating around big issues.

Badmouthing

Don't badmouth your ex or his or her new partner. No one really wants to hear you dwell on his or her personality defects, failings and appalling habits. What is the point? If the relationship is over you are prolonging the fallout by continually saying negative things about your ex. Of course there's going to be an initial anger and you will want to discuss the break-up around the time it happened. After that you are hurting yourself if you engage in badmouthing in front of your children, family and friends. Not alone are you damaging yourself but you're being rude and boring. There is nothing less interesting than starting a conversation with a new person that immediately turns into a bitching session about their ex.

If you meet a lawyer socially you really shouldn't start into a long description of your legal travails. The lawyer hears that kind of stuff all day every day in work and doesn't need to hear it during down time. It's as rude as asking a dentist to give you a free examination of your bad tooth during a dinner party, and you wouldn't do that, would you?

If your ex is badmouthing you, you can only ask him or her politely to stop. After that, maintain your dignity. If you respond you're letting yourself down and the people who are important in your life, who know you well, will know that it's not true. If the badmouthing gets out of control and becomes malicious contact your lawyer for advice on defamation.

New Partners and Step-Parenting

Your relationship with your ex's new partner or your new partner's relationship with your ex can be a huge source of conflict in relation to your joint parenting. If you are the parent who does most of the caring for the children (often the mother) and your ex has a new girlfriend or wife your relationship can be tumultuous. As a father it can be equally galling to see a new man entering your child's life and doing activities with him or her that you consider your role.

How can you minimise conflict in this situation? It takes a lot of hard work and determination from both sides to make these complicated parenting arrangements work smoothly. Some of the things you may need to consider are discussed below.

- Don't take animosity personally. You are not hated or despised. It is what you represent that upsets the other person. Think about it. If you met your ex's new partner in an ordinary social situation you would have no reason to hate or mistrust each other. It's the dynamic of your relationship that causes the conflict. Maybe you're fighting over shared resources (such as money) or time with the children. It's important to keep your focus on what your shared goals are, which should be your children and what is best for them.

- If your ex had an affair and you think the new partner was responsible for the break-up of your relationship it's going to be hard to get along. You have to go through the stages of grieving for your old relationship and anger towards your ex and their new partner is part of that. If you maintain the anger into the future you are only hurting yourself because it's really not going to affect them. You don't necessarily have to forgive and respect your ex and his or her new partner immediately but you do have to let go of the negative angry feelings you have towards them. If you hold on to those feelings they will consume and damage you. If you're finding it impossible to control your anger then a psychotherapist or cognitive behavioural therapist can help you overcome your negative feelings through talk therapy or by keeping a diary or record of your thoughts.

- Assuming you can let go of your anger and communicate rationally with your ex, treat your ex as you would like to be treated. Imagine the situation from your own perspective before you make a decision. For example, if you have a new partner and he or she is moving in with you and your children, or you are planning a holiday together, think about how you would feel if the situation was reversed. Would you like to be told about the role the new partner was assuming in your children's lives? Of course you would. Just because you have a bad history with your ex doesn't mean you can't start treating him or her with respect and tolerance at any stage.

- Try to imagine what you would like the relationship between you and your co-parent and others who are involved in parenting your children to be like and work hard to achieve your ideal. If you would like open and honest communication be open and honest yourself and ask for it in response. If you want good timekeeping be a good timekeeper yourself. If you're finding it hard to communicate with your ex you can try to communicate with your ex's new partner. Sometimes an open conversation over a cup of coffee with your ex's new partner can achieve a shift in your relationship.

- Think carefully before you introduce a new partner into your children's lives. If they are very young you don't want them hurt and confused so timing and preparation are very important. Wait until you're sure that the person is going to be important in your life.

- Stand back and don't intrude on parenting. If the children aren't your own then you have to take a back seat and let the children's parents be responsible for disciplining their children. Your role is to be supportive but you can't interfere unless you have built up a strong relationship with the children over a long time.

- You cannot change the behaviour of others. You can only change your own behaviour and reactions to others. You can praise a new partner or step-parent, you can stand back and show respect, and you can cooperate and ask for help.

- Don't expect instant love from stepchildren. They might resent you for taking time away from their time with their parent and not appreciate anything you do for them. It takes time to build up relationships with stepchildren. It's good to stand back and give it time. Jumping in and trying to do everything for them won't give you an instant relationship with them. It happens slowly, so be patient.

- If you are genuinely worried that the behaviour of a new partner is seriously dangerous or detrimental to the health, safety or welfare of your children of course you must take action. In those circumstances you will have to seek help from the relevant professionals – social workers, lawyers, healthcare professionals or your GP.

The Legal Status of Step-Parents in Ireland

At present Irish law only recognises two people as capable of being parents with rights to custody, guardianship and access. You become a step-parent when you become fully involved in parenting your partner's children either by cohabiting, registering a civil partnership or remarrying, but as a step-parent you don't have any legal rights towards your partner's children. If your relationship ends you can be ordered to pay maintenance for your partner's children under certain circumstances. For example, if you lived with them or married your partner and assumed financial responsibility for their children.

Step-parents can apply to adopt children they are parenting in very limited circumstances. They must be married to the parent of the child and the application must be made by both spouses together. The natural parent and the new step-parent apply together so that the natural parent's rights aren't extinguished.

The most common situation in which step-parenting adoption takes place is where the natural mother has married and the natural father isn't in the picture. The natural parent gives up his or her legal rights and responsibilities in relation to his or her child and the new spouse takes on parental responsibility with all the legal rights that flow from that to the child.

The adopted stepchild then has the same legal status as any other child of the family, such as in matters of inheritance, guardianship, maintenance and a new surname. If the child is over seven years of age there is a process of consultation under Irish law. Every child being considered for adoption has to have an age appropriate understanding of the process during the family's assessment for the adoption with the Adoption Board.

The other natural parent (usually the birth father) must be notified of the application for adoption and if he is a guardian his consent has to be obtained. It's difficult to go ahead with the adoption if the natural father is involved with his child and objects to the adoption. Once the child is adopted by the natural parent and step-parent the original parent's rights (usually the father's) are extinguished.

A step-parent may not apply for guardianship if he or she is a cohabitant, civil partner or spouse of a natural parent. The Law Reform Commission recommended in its *Report on the Legal Aspects of Family Relationships* that parental responsibility should be extended to step-parents and civil partners by an agreement or by application to court. This would mean that children could have an increased number of adults taking parental responsibility for them.

Special Occasions

Weddings, funerals, graduations, Christmas, birthdays and other special occasions need to be handled with sensitivity and caution when you have a complicated family situation after a divorce or separation.

If you and your ex have children and the event is focused on your child then you both should concentrate on making sure it goes smoothly. If your ex insists or wants to invite his or her new partner and the event is important to your child then you must make an effort to be civil and polite in their company. You don't have to sit beside them or have a long conversation with them if you're not comfortable but you should put aside your feelings and attend for the sake of your child.

If you're attending a family event, like a Christmas lunch with your children or a child's birthday, it can be nicer for the child if you both come alone. If you think that it might be awkward for your family to bring along your new partner then ask your new partner not to attend. There's no point in ruining an occasion because you want your new partner to be included in everything. Ask your children if they want it to be 'family only' and agree with your ex to leave your new partner(s) behind if the children are happier with that.

As a new partner you should never assume that you're going to be invited to everything. If you're in a long-term second relationship and very involved with your partner's children you still shouldn't expect to be automatically included in everything. There will be some times when the child will have events that will only include his or her parents.

When children are older it is up to them to decide who they want to invite. If you are excluded from a wedding/party/graduation then don't take it personally. Family events are tricky enough and you are better off not being in the firing line. There will be other less stressful, more appropriate occasions that will give you the opportunity to interact positively with your new partner's children.

New Friends and Dating

Many people who are married or in long-term relationships spend a huge amount of time together. If you have children your social life can become curtailed because of joint parental responsibility; you may have lost contact with your single friends and be spending more time with couples with children the same age as your own. If your relationship was going badly you may have become isolated from your friends or family because you found it difficult to talk to them or you were trying to hide the effects of the relationship breakdown.

The end of your relationship can leave a huge gap in your social life. Some of your joint friends will invariably take sides, and both you and your ex may find yourselves losing contact with family members and friends who are closer to one or other of you. If you are on your own you may lose contact with couples who are uncomfortable spending time with you as a single person. It's hard to go out with a group of couples as the only one without a partner, especially if you are particularly sad immediately after your break-up.

It may feel strange and unnatural to have to think about going out and making new friends or actively dating again if you're older and have already settled into a routine. The idea of having to 'go out there' and meet new people, date and sleep with someone you don't know can be enough to keep some couples together or bring them back together again.

You don't have to meet new people or have a new partner but mental health professionals are unanimous in their opinion that having contact with people – friends and family – is essential for your mental health and well-being. Being completely alone isn't good for anyone.

If you have no difficulty meeting people and go through life making friends and enjoying your friend-ships then your active social life is probably due to your personality and attitude. Friendly, open people who are interested in others will invariably meet new people and make friends easily. Opportunities to meet people arise all the time and it's really up to you to make the best of every social event or occasion when you have contact with new people.

It's difficult to date and meet new people when you're in the middle of your divorce or separation. It's usually better to wait until things have settled down, you have sorted out any issues and your living arrangements are stable before you embark on dating or a new relationship. Fate can sometimes take over and you might meet someone you are very attracted to when you're in the middle of the storm, but if you're really preoccupied with your break-up you won't be in the frame of mind to get involved.

If you have fully analysed the reason your relationship ended you may have discovered that it was due to a problem that you have with relationships or yourself. Now is the time to deal with that problem. If your co-dependency, drug or alcohol abuse, insecurity, neediness or other problem caused or contributed to your relationship failure then there is always the danger that you will bring your difficulties into a new relationship.

Take time to think about your past relationships. Is there a pattern? Do you need to go to a therapist to analyse or discover the reasons for your difficulties? It's easy to blame your ex for the failure of your relationship but if he or she was dysfunctional you ought to think about why you chose to have a relationship with a dysfunctional person. If he or she was unfaithful or an alcoholic were you aware that the propensity was there when you married or lived together? Did you accept unacceptable behaviour during the relationship?

Self-examination with the help of a therapist is very useful before you embark on dating again. Feedback from friends and family who have witnessed your dating and relationship history first-hand can be illuminating too.

Often people close to us can clearly spot the reasons for our mistakes; unfortunately it's very difficult to hear and accept their opinions and it's not easy to tell someone if you think they're about to make a bad decision. You are an adult and it's unrealistic to put blame on your family and friends for not telling you that they always thought you were heading for disaster when you decided to move in with your lover, got married, registered your civil partnership or had a child with someone they really didn't think was right for you.

There are absolutely no hard and fast rules about how you can meet new people or ask people out on dates. Everyone has their own unique approach. The following are suggestions of activities that will bring you into contact with new people. After that it's up to you! Even if you're not very interested in a particular activity there's nothing wrong with giving it a try.

Clubs, Pubs and Wine Bars

Clubs, pubs and wine bars probably aren't the best places to meet people. When large groups of people are drinking alcohol the atmosphere can be chaotic. However, in Ireland a lot of social activity does take place in pubs, clubs and wine bars, and you can meet new people during a night out, so this approach can be successful. Just be careful that you don't run into danger. Mixing alcohol and socialising with strangers can spell disaster. A casual encounter might be the start of a great relationship but if you're inebriated in the company of a person you don't know you might find yourself having a casual sexual encounter with someone who is married or in a relationship. At worst you might be putting yourself in danger of being raped, being accused of raping someone or being infected with a disease.

Further Education

Evening classes or college courses are a great way of meeting people. If you studied at third level before your break-up you probably made lots of friends while you were pursuing your education. These days most jobs and professions have some sort of continuing education, so unless your job is overwhelmingly made up of one sex (unfortunately you're unlikely to meet a woman on a building site or a man at a beauty therapy course) you can do a course that's linked to your job and meet new people at the same time.

Evening classes are fun if you think they're going to be useful to you. Again don't take a course that's going to be full of men or women. If you're a man or a woman inter-ested in meeting women you'll meet lots of them in certain classes – languages and yoga for example – and men are more interested in doing a motor maintenance courses than women. So before you book into a class make sure that it has the type of people you want to meet in the class.

Use Your Contacts

Your friends and family are a great resource. They know you well and if you tell them you're lonely or interested in meeting someone new they'll keep an eye out for you. They can invite people they think you might get along with to an event or organise a blind date for you. Your friends and family can include you in their social events if you ask them. Get more involved with your nephews and nieces; kids are a great icebreaker. Offer to exercise a horse, walk a dog, pick up kids from school, or help out with sporting events and dinner parties. If you volunteer to help out and are enthusiastic you will be included and introduced to new people.

Sporting Activities

Joining a gym or taking up a new sporting activity is another way of meeting people. If you're going to the same exercise classes or training at the same time every week you're sure to meet new people. You'll know that they're interested in sports and keeping fit. Again if you want to meet people of the same or opposite sex there's no point in going to certain gym classes or sporting activities that will be predominantly of one or other sex. The added advantage of going to a gym is that you can be there on your own and have a one-on-one conversation without feeling awkward.

Mixed team sports such as tag rugby are becoming more popular and if you join a cycling, golf, horse riding, motor sports or tennis club with social evenings you're sure to meet some new people. There is an endless array of sports to get involved in, so you are bound to find something that interests you, whether it's walking, trekking, surfing or sea kayaking, or extreme sports such as skydiving, hang gliding, paragliding or parachuting.

General Social Activities

There are meet-up groups for people who like to do certain activities or go out to social events together. There are dance groups, choirs, craft and reading groups, wine, poetry, art and music appreciation societies, and motor car, motorbike, walking, hiking, gardening and food-based groups and activities. You could take dancing, pottery or art classes. The internet is a great place to look for these types of groups in your local area. Just Google the things that interest you and you are sure to find something.

Faith-Based or Volunteering Activities

Your local church, mosque, synagogue or other faith-based group will always have social activities for its members. Even if you have fallen away from your religion you might find it a comfort at this time. Volunteering to help out with elderly, homeless or young people can cheer you up by helping you to focus on others instead of your own problems. There are websites for charities and non-governmental organisations in the resources section of this book which are always looking for volunteers and there are volunteering websites such as <u>volunteeringireland.ie</u> and <u>volunteer.ie</u> that will try to match your skills and location to suitable volunteering opportunities for you.

Group Travel

Going to conferences and travelling with groups is a great way of making new friends. If you get on with people after the pressure of being abroad on a trip then you're likely to stay friends. You'll always have an adventure when you're travelling and your shared experience can provide a solid start to a relationship.

Don't be afraid to go away on your own. It's easy to play it safe and travel abroad with friends but it's very hard to experience a new country if you're filtering it through others. Being alone will force you to make contact with new people and try to speak the language. Make sure you're safe; if you want to travel without friends it's better to go with an organised group or stay in suitable places so that you're not vulnerable.

Travel companies organise holidays that are specifically child free or for singles so check out the profile of the group or hotel with your travel agent when you're booking. There are charitable organisations that set up trips to other countries to raise money for specific projects. There are also eco-friendly holidays where you can work on a farm or in a cooperative setting in return for accommodation. Travelling with a specific purpose can be very interesting and rewarding and if there are others who are on the trip with the same purpose you will probably find that you have a lot in common.

Internet Dating

If you are connected (and we're all supposed to be) just Google 'internet dating in Ireland' and lots of internet dating websites will come up. There is a perception that internet dating is full of sad, strange and desperate people who can't meet anyone in the real world, but in reality it is just another forum that many ordinary people use to befriend and meet new people with similar interests. Internet dating is a growing phenomenon in Ireland and there are hundreds of thousands of people registered on sites such as <u>Match.com</u>, <u>Anotherfriend.com</u> and <u>Maybefriends.com</u>. If you are comfortable with the idea of using an internet dating service and are planning to post your profile online so that you can chat and possibly meet new people you ought to use good judgement and take the following advice:

- Use a well-known and reputable website. Make sure that you check and are comfortable with the privacy settings for all your communications and information.

- Be careful. Remain anonymous until you're sure you want to give out any details about yourself. Don't put anything personal that might identify you, your children, your house or your workplace on your profile.

- If you're communicating with someone you like online ask them questions. If their answers are strange, inconsistent or make you feel uncomfortable then cease communications.

- Arrange a phone conversation if you think you might like the person. Don't give them your mobile number – give them an anonymous or Skype number that you are comfortable using for your initial contact.

- If you arrange to meet someone you've only communicated with over the internet make sure you pick somewhere that is public and safe, and where you are known. Let your friends or family know that you're going on a date with someone you don't know. Take your mobile phone and make sure you have a safe way of getting home.

- Trust your instincts. If you get a bad vibe from the person leave. Don't allow yourself to be manipulated or persuaded to stay if you're really not comfortable.

- Married people or those in civil partnerships may go online and pretend to be single. Don't fall into the trap of getting close to someone before you know for sure that they are not in a relationship.

Conclusion

*'The Chinese use two brush strokes to write the word "crisis".
One brush stroke stands for danger; the other for opportunity. In a
crisis be aware of the danger – but recognise the opportunity.' –
John F. Kennedy*

While you're going through a break-up it can feel as if your life is in crisis. It's important to try to stand back and recognise that a crisis can also be a positive event if you can use it as an opportunity to learn. If you have gone through the process of making decisions and dealing with the logistics after your relationship breakdown now might be the time to reflect on the past and think about your future.

Many things contribute to relationship breakdown and often it's a mixture of different problems and stresses. It's not always a simple matter of blaming one person or identifying one issue. It's complicated. People and couples have problems: they make poor choices; they are vulnerable and have addictions or problems with fidelity and alcohol abuse; they suffer from mental health problems, personality disorders, financial problems or poor parenting skills.

If you have had any of these problems in your relationships in the past now is the time to think about how to eliminate them from your future. Take time and use the advice in the resources and further reading sections of this book to help you to find more information that will give you the strength to cope with your life after your relationship breakdown.

Don't be disappointed if you can't solve your problems in the way you want to. Mediation doesn't always work out and the legal system doesn't always guarantee a fair outcome. You may have to accept that you can't persuade your ex to adhere to your children's parenting plan and if your ex has a mental health or addiction problem or a personality disorder and won't go for help you may have to find a way to cope with it rather than cure it.

Nothing is ever perfect and your aim should be to improve your situation to the best of your ability. Certain things will always be outside your control and if you're still finding it difficult to accept your situation then counselling might help.

Remind yourself of what you need to know when things aren't going according to plan. Read other books that are relevant to your particular problem and look for more information if the problem isn't being resolved. Don't judge yourself harshly and keep going over what you did wrong in the past. Now is the time to move on and allow yourself to put your mistakes behind you. The most important thing to remember is that if you don't learn from your past and you allow it to define you, you will miss out on many interesting and exciting possibilities in your future.

Further Reading

Self-Help

- *Alcoholics Anonymous: The Big Book* by AA Services, Hazelden Information and Educational Services.
- *Be Excellent at Anything* by Tony Schwartz, Jean Gomes and Catherine McCarthy, Simon and Schuster.
- *Coming through Depression: A Mindful Approach to Recovery* by Tony Bates, Newleaf
- *Counselling Survivors of Domestic Abuse* by Christiane Sanderson, Jessica Kingsley Publishers.
- *Depression: The Common Sense Approach* by Tony Bates, Newleaf.
- *Divorce Poison: How to Protect Your Family from Badmouthing and Brainwashing* by Richard Warshak, Harper.
- *Eight Keys to Safe Trauma Recovery: Take-Charge Strategies to Empower Your Healing* by Babette Rothschild, W.W. Norton and Co.
- *Emotional Intelligence* by Daniel Goleman, Bloomsbury.
- *The Feeling Good Handbook* by David Burns, Plume.
- *Flourishing* by Maureen Gaffney, Penguin Ireland.
- *Getting the Love You Want, Keeping the Love You Find* by Harville Hendrix, Pocket Books.

- *The Happiness Project* by Gretchen Rubin, Harper.
- *It Works: How and Why – The Twelve Steps and Twelve Traditions of Narcotics Anonymous* by Narcotics Anonymous, NAWS Inc.
- *Men Are from Mars, Women Are from Venus* by John Gray, Harper Collins.
- *The Mindful Way through Depression* by Mark Williams, John Teasdale, Zindel Segal and Jon Kabat-Zinn, The Guilford Press.
- *Narcotics Anonymous* by Narcotics Anonymous, Hazelden Information and Educational Services.
- *The Optimum Nutrition Bible* by Patrick Holford, Piatkus.
- *The Seven Habits of Highly Effective People: Powerful Lessons in Personal Change* by Stephen Covey, Simon and Schuster.
- *Social Intelligence* by Daniel Goleman, Bloomsbury.
- *Twelve Steps and Twelve Traditions* by AA Services, Hazelden Information and Educational Services.
- *The Verbally Abusive Relationship* by Patricia Evans, Adams Media.
- *What to Eat? Ten Chewy Questions About Daily Food and Drink* by Hattie Ellis, Granta.

Parenting and Children

- *All About Children: Questions Parents Ask* by Tony Humphreys, Newleaf.
- *Annabel Karmel's New Complete Baby and Toddler Meal Planner* by Annabel Karmel, Ebury Press.
- *Babyproofing Your Marriage* by Stacie Cockrell, Cathy O'Neill and Julia Stone, HarperCollins.
- *Children's Rights in Ireland: Law, Policy and Practice* by Ursula Kilkelly, Tottel Publishing.

- *Children Are from Heaven: Positive Parenting Skills for Raising Cooperative, Confident and Compassionate Children* by John Gray, Quill.
- *The Everything Guide to Stepparenting* by Erin Munroe and Irene Levine, Adams Media.
- *Family Law Practitioner: Children and the Law* by Geoffrey Shannon, Round Hall.
- *How To Talk so Kids Will Listen and Listen so Kids Will Talk* by Adele Faber and Elaine Mazlish, Picadilly Press Ltd.
- *Parenting Is Child's Play* by David Coleman, Penguin Ireland.
- *Parenting Is Child's Play: The Teenage Years* by David Coleman, Penguin Ireland.
- *The Politics of Children's Rights* by Frank Martin and Carol Coulter, Cork University Press.
- *Raising Boys* by Steve Biddulp, Harper Thorsons.
- *Siblings Without Rivalry* by Adele Faber and Elaine Mazlish, William Morrow Paperbacks.
- *What to Expect: The First Year* by Heidi Murkoff with Sharon Mazel, Simon and Schuster.
- *What to Expect: The Toddler Years* by Heidi Murkoff with Sharon Mazel, Simon and Schuster.
- *Your Baby and Child* by Penelope Leach, Dorling Kindersley.

Conflict Resolution

- *The Art of Mediation* by Michele Hermann, NITA.
- *Beyond Winning: Negotiating to Create Value in Deals and Disputes* by Robert Mnookin, Scott Peppet and Andrew Tulumello, Belknap Press.
- *Divorce and Separation* by Rosy Border and Jane Moir, Cavendish Publishing.

- *The Dynamics of Conflict Resolution* by Bernard Mayer, Jossey-Bass.
- *Ex-Etiquette for Parents: Good Behavior After a Divorce or Separation* by Jann Blackstone-Ford and Sharyl Jupe, Chicago Review Press.
- *The Fundamentals of Family Mediation* by John Haynes, State University of New York Press.
- *Getting Past No: Negotiating in Difficult Situations* by William Ury, Random House Publishing Group.
- *Getting to Yes: Negotiating Agreement Without Giving In* by Roger Fisher, William Ury and Bruce Patton, Penguin Group (USA).
- *Mediating Dangerously* by Kenneth Cloke, Jossey-Bass.
- *The Mediation Process: Practical Strategies for Resolving Conflict* by Christopher Moore, Jossey-Bass.
- *The Mediator's Handbook* by Jennifer Beer and Eileen Stief, New Society Publisher.
- *The Promise of Mediation* by Robert Baruch Bush and Joseph Folger, Jossey-Bass.

Legal and Financial

- *Bonnie's Household Budget Book* by Bonnie McCullough, St Martin's Griffin.
- *The Common Cents Money Management Workbook* by Judy Lawrence, Kaplan.
- *The Complete Guide to Protecting Your Financial Security When Getting a Divorce* by Alan Feigenbaum and Heather Linton, McGraw Hill.
- *Divorce in Ireland* by Kieron Wood and Paul O'Shea, second edition, First Law.
- *Family Law* by Louise Crowley, Thomson Round Hall.

- *Family Law* (Law Society of Ireland Manuals) by Geoffrey Shannon, fourth edition, Oxford University Press.
- *Family Law in Practice: A Study of Cases in the Circuit Court* by Carol Coulter, Clarus Press.
- *Family Law Negotiations* by Kevin Liston, Round Hall.
- *An Introduction to Irish Family Law* by Jim Nestor, fourth edition, Gill and Macmillan.
- *The Irish Family Law Handbook* by Deirdre Kennedy and Elizabeth Maguire, fourth edition, Bloomsbury Professional.
- *Irish Journal of Family Law* edited by Geoffrey Shannon, Round Hall.
- *The Irish Legal System* by Dorothy Donovan, Round Hall.
- *Shatter's Family Law* by Alan Shatter, fourth edition, Tottel Publishing.
- *Thrifty Ways for Modern Days* by Martin Lewis, Vermillion.

Resources

The author supplies the following information in relation to the organisations listed below from their websites and cannot ensure the accuracy of the information. She does not endorse the products or services supplied by any of the organisations.

ACCORD

Accord is a voluntary Catholic organisation that aims to promote a deeper understanding of Christian marriage and to offer people the means to safeguard and nourish their family relationships. It provides marriage and relationship counselling services and marriage preparation programmes and has 58 local centres.
Accord Central Office, Columba Centre, Maynooth, Co. Kildare; www.accord.ie; 01-5053112; admin@accord.ie

AIM FAMILY SERVICES

AIM is a voluntary organisation that offers non-denominational couple and individual counselling, family mediation and a legal information service to people experiencing marital, relationship and family problems.

AIM, 64 Dame Street, Dublin 2; www.aimfamilyservices.ie; 01-6708363; aimfamilyservices@eircom.net

AL-ANON AND ALATEEN

The purpose of Al-Anon is to help families and friends of alcoholics recover from the effects of living with the problem drinking of a relative or friend in an anonymous environment. It is not affiliated with any other organisation or outside entity. Alateen is part of the Al-Anon fellowship and is for young people aged 12–17 inclusive. *Al-Anon Information Centre, Room 5, 5 Capel Street, Dublin 1; www.al-anon-ireland.org; 01-8732699; info@al-anon-ireland.org*

ALCOHOL ACTION IRELAND

Alcohol Action Ireland is the national charity for alcohol-related issues. It provides information on alcohol-related issues, creates awareness of alcohol-related harm and offers potential policy solutions for reducing that harm. *Alcohol Action Ireland, Butler Court, 25 Great Strand Street, Dublin 1; alcoholireland.ie; 01-8780610; info@alcoholactionireland.ie*

ALCOHOLICS ANONYMOUS

Alcoholics Anonymous is a fellowship of men and women who share their experience, strength and hope with each other so that they may solve their common problem and help each other to recover from alcoholism. The only requirement for membership is a desire to stop drinking. There are no dues or fees and it is not allied with any sect, denomination, politics, organisation or institution; it

does not wish to engage in any controversy, and it neither endorses not opposes any cause. The primary purpose of its members is to stay sober and help other alcoholics achieve sobriety.
General Service Office of Alcoholics Anonymous, Unit 2, Block C, Santry Business Park, Swords Road, Dublin 9; www.alcoholicsanonymous.ie; 01-8420700; gso@ alcoholicsanonymous.ie

AMEN

Amen is a voluntary group, founded in 1997. It provides a confidential helpline, support groups, legal advice, counselling and court accompaniment for male victims of domestic abuse and their children. Thousands of men and supportive members of their families have contacted it since it was set up.
AMEN, St Anne's Resource Centre, Railway Street, Navan, Co. Meath; www.amen.ie; 046-9023718; info@amen.ie

AMNESTY INTERNATIONAL IRELAND

Amnesty International Ireland is Ireland's largest human rights organisation and part of a global movement of over 3.2 million people working in more than 150 countries. It campaigns for victims of torture and state-sponsored violence. In Ireland it campaigns for improvement in the lives of people who experience mental health difficulties and for equality in Irish law for lesbian, gay, bisexual and transgender people. It is an independent organisation and is concerned with the protection of fundamental human rights guaranteed to each one of us by the Universal Declaration of Human Rights.

Amnesty International Ireland, Sean MacBride House, 48 Fleet Street, Dublin 2; www.amnesty.ie; 01-8638300; info@ amnesty.ie

ANA LIFFEY DRUG PROJECT

The ALDP is a drug project based in Dublin's inner city. Its mission is to work with people affected by problem substance abuse and it aims to reduce harm, improve overall quality of life and promote human rights. It neither promotes nor denounces problem substance use and believes in the importance of journeying with people. It envisions that everyone affected by problem substance abuse has a right to health, dignity and respect.
Ana Liffey Drug Project, 48 Middle Abbey Street, Dublin 1; www.aldp.ie; 01-8786899; info@aldp.ie

THE ARK

The Ark is Europe's first custom-built children's cultural centre. It programmes, promotes and hosts high quality cultural work which is by children, for children and about children. It is a charitable organisation, founded on the principle that all children as citizens have the same cultural entitlements as adults. It works with a diverse range of Irish and international artists to develop original, inspirational and playful programmes for children so they can extend their imaginations and horizons.
The Ark, 11a Eustace Street, Temple Bar, Dublin 2; www.ark. ie; 01-6707788; boxoffice@ark.ie

ASSOCIATION FOR PSYCHOANALYSIS AND PSYCHOTHERAPY IN IRELAND

The APPI started in 1993 as an informal group made up largely of graduates of clinical psychotherapy at St Vincent's University Hospital. It is now a professional organisation that facilitates registration and accreditation of its members. It organises an annual congress, its members are very involved in teaching and it has an academic journal. Graduates of Master's programmes in Psychotherapy at St Vincent's University Hospital and graduates of the Masters degree in Psychoanalysis at LSB College and DBS are eligible for membership of the APPI. *www.appi.ie*

ASSOCIATION OF COLLABORATIVE PRACTITIONERS

The ACP is a limited liability company with members comprising lawyers, personal and family professionals (including psychotherapists, psychologists, counsellors and mediators) and financial specialists whose aim is to promote collaborative practice among those disciplines as an alternative means of dispute resolution in family separation and divorce and other areas. The participants in the group have trained with leading proponents of the collaborative model including Pauline Tesler. Its aims are to promote collaborative law as a dispute resolution mechanism, support practitioners by providing information and ethical guidelines, and provide training and peer review structures for practitioners. The names of lawyers and other experts are accessible through its website. *www.acp.ie*

AWARE

Aware is a voluntary organisation that provides support for people with depression. Its mission is to create a society where people with depression and their families are understood and supported, are free from stigma and have access to a broad range of appropriate therapies to enable them to reach their full potential. Its aim is to educate the public in relation to depression, provide emotional and practical support to those affected and to support research into the treatment of depression.

Aware, National Office, 72 Lower Leeson Street, Dublin 2; www.aware.ie; 01-6617211; info@aware.ie

BAR COUNCIL OF IRELAND

The Bar Council of Ireland regulates the professional practice of barristers, is responsible for the membership of the Law Library and maintains the facilities of those barristers who practise from the Law Library. The website of the Bar Council provides access to a list of its members and their qualifications, a list of mediators and their qualifications, a voluntary assistance scheme and details of its complaints procedure.

The Bar Council Administration Office, Four Courts, Dublin 7; www.lawlibrary.ie; 01-8175000; barcouncil@lawlibrary.ie

BARNARDOS

The work of Barnardos is child focused. It aims to provide practical and professional support to children and to bring hope into situations where hope is sometimes lost. It has 40 community-based centres, national services and links with partner organisations. It offers a variety of specialised services such as bereavement counselling, guardian *ad litem*, origins tracing, post adoption advice, an intergenerational reading programme, childcare contact centres and vetting services for groups and organisations involved in childcare. It campaigns and lobbies to protect the rights of children and influence government and decision makers and offers training courses to parents and people who work with children.

Barnardos National Office, Christchurch Square, Dublin 8; www.barnardos.ie; 01-4530355, Callsave 1850-222300; info@barnardos.ie

BELONG TO

Belong To is an organisation for lesbian, gay, bisexual and transgendered (LGBT) young people aged between 14 and 23. It believes that LGBT young people need to be respected and cared for on the same basis as all young people and when they are safe and supported in their families, schools and society they will thrive as healthy and equal citizens. It provides direct youth work services to young people and support to youth groups all around the country. It works with teachers, youth workers, youth services and government departments to change negative societal attitudes and to ensure that positive social changes occur.

Belong To, Parliament House, 13 Parliament Street, Dublin 2; www.belongto.org; 01-6706223; info@belongto.org

BODYWHYS

Bodywhys is the Eating Disorders Association of Ireland. It is a national voluntary organisation dedicated to supporting people in Ireland affected by eating disorders.

It provides a range of support services for people who are affected by eating disorders, including specific services for families and friends. Its vision is that people affected by eating disorders will have their needs met through the provision of an appropriate, integrated quality service delivered by a range of statutory, private and voluntary agencies. It has a helpline, resources and a support group, and provides information on treatment options.

Bodywhys – The Eating Disorders Association of Ireland, PO Box 105, Blackrock, Co. Dublin; www.bodywhys.ie; 01-2834963, Helpline 1890-200444; info@bodywhys.ie, Support: alex@bodywhys.ie

CARI

CARI is a charity founded in 1989. Its aim is to provide professional child-centred therapy and counselling services to children, families and groups affected by child sexual abuse. It also aims to provide up-to-date education and information for children, adults and professionals on the dynamics of child abuse and to raise public and political awareness.

The CARI Foundation, National Office, 110 Lower Drumcondra Road, Dublin 9; www.cari.ie; 01-8308529, Helpline 1890-924567; helpline@cari.ie, info@cari.ie

CATHOLIC YOUTH CARE

Catholic Youth Care is a leading provider of youth services in Dublin. It provides direct youth work in ten local services and support for voluntary youth work. Its mission is to promote a youth work response that is caring, compassionate and Christian and enables young people to participate more fully in the life of society and the Catholic Church. Its youth services have adventure clubs, crime diversion projects, summer projects, youth clubs and information centres. It also organises retreats and pilgrimages.

Catholic Youth Care, Head Office, Catholic Youth Care, Arran Quay, Dublin 7; www.cyc.ie; 01-8725055

CHILDLINE

Childline is part of the Irish Society for the Prevention of Cruelty to Children. It is a charity that has a telephone service, online service and texting service for children who want to talk about any problems they might be worried about or who are looking for information. The organisation also gives talks on and campaigns for children's rights. Its website provides information on lots of issues that affect children.

www.childline.ie; 1800-666666

CHILDMINDING IRELAND

Childminding Ireland is a charity founded by a group of childminders and is now the national body for childminders. Childminders can register with Childminding Ireland and avail of its information and training. Parents who need a childminder can use its vacancy matching service.

Childminding Ireland, Unit 9, Bulford Business Campus, Kilcoole, Co. Wicklow; www.childminding.ie; 01-2878466; info@childminding.ie

CHILDREN IN HOSPITAL IN IRELAND

Children in Hospital in Ireland is a voluntary organisation that is committed to promoting and ensuring the welfare of all children in hospital and their families. It has been working directly to bring fun and support to sick children for over 40 years. It uses its expertise to deliver daily and weekly play sessions that support child patients, parents and staff in 20 hospital wards and playrooms nationwide.

Children in Hospital Ireland, Carmichael Centre, Coleraine House, Coleraine Street, Dublin 7; www.childreninhospital.ie; 1890-252682; info@childreninhospital.ie

CHILDREN'S RIGHTS ALLIANCE

The Children's Rights Alliance is a coalition of over 90 non-governmental organisations working to secure the rights and needs of children in Ireland by campaigning for the full implementation of the UN Convention on the Rights of the Child. It aims to improve the lives of all children under 18 through securing the necessary changes in Ireland's laws, policies and services.

Children's Rights Alliance, 4 Upper Mount Street, Dublin 2; www.childrensrights.ie; 01-6629400; info@childrensrights.ie

CITIZENS INFORMATION BOARD

The Citizens Information Board is a statutory government body that provides information, advice and advocacy on a broad range of public and social services. It provides an Irish eGovernment website and supports the voluntary network of Citizens Information Centres and phone services. The website is very useful as it provides comprehensive information on public services and the entitlements of citizens in Ireland. It gathers information from government departments and agencies and presents

it in an easy to understand way. There are 260 locations nationwide.
www.citizensinformationboard.ie, www.citizensinformation.ie;
076-1074000

COLLEGE OF PSYCHIATRY OF IRELAND

The College of Psychiatry is the professional body for psychiatrists in Ireland and is the sole body recognised by the Medical Council and the HSE for competence assurance and training in psychiatry. It offers membership to psychiatrists and trainees. The members are all qualified doctors who have completed further training. The college aims to address relevant issues for its members, psychiatry in general, mental health services and service users. It supports *A Vision for Change* and urges the government to ensure it will be implemented in full so that Ireland will have the mental health service it deserves.
The College of Psychiatry Ireland, 5 Herbert Street, Dublin 2; www.irishpsychiatry.ie; 01-6618450; info@irishpsychiatry.ie

CONSOLE

Console is a charity that provides a national Freephone helpline which is a confidential listening service operated by a team of counsellors. It aims to provide support, advice and referral services to anyone bereaved by suicide. It offers local support groups and training programmes on suicide studies, and promotes public awareness of suicide prevention and the reduction of the stigma surrounding suicide.
Console, Console House, 4 Whitethorn Grove, Celbridge, Co. Kildare; www.console.ie; 01-6102638, Helpline 1800-201890; info@console.ie

COPE GALWAY

COPE Galway is a local Galway charity that provides services to those isolated in the community. It provides sustenance and social supports to older people, a refuge for women and children affected by domestic violence and accommodation for men and women experiencing homelessness.

COPE Galway, 2–5 Calbro House, Tuam Road, Galway; www. copegalway.ie; 091-778750; info@copegalway.ie

COURTS SERVICE OF IRELAND

The Courts Service manages the courts, supports the judiciary and provides a high quality and professional service to all users of the courts. It provides information on the courts system to the public, provides, manages and maintains the court buildings and provides facilities to the users of the courts. Its website provides lots of information, including forms, the legal diary, rules and fees, guidance on procedure, judgments, publications and statistics.

The Courts Service, 15–24 Phoenix Street North, Smithfield, Dublin 7; www.courts.ie; 01-8886000

CRISIS PREGNANCY PROGRAMME

The HSE Crisis Pregnancy Programme aims to develop and implement a national strategy to address the issue of crisis pregnancy in Ireland. Its core objectives are a reduction in the number of crisis pregnancies by the provision of education, advice and contraceptive services; a reduction in the number of women with crisis pregnancies who opt for abortion by offering services and supports which make other options more attractive; and the provision of counselling services, medical services and such other health services for the purpose of providing support, after crisis pregnancy, as it deems appropriate.

HSE Crisis Pregnancy Programme, Fourth Floor, 89–94 Capel Street, Dublin 1; www.crisispregnancy.ie; 01-8146292; info@crisispregnancy.ie

CROSSCARE

Crosscare provides homeless services, a night service to people sleeping on the streets, community services and young people's services. It was formerly known as the Catholic Social Service Conference and has been responding to the needs of people on the margins of society since 1941. It has a diverse range of programmes and reaches into areas of high need. It has a number of projects that provide emergency accommodation to adults and children, help for Travellers and immigrants, disability awareness, food initiatives, drug and alcohol programmes, teen counselling, and community training and education.

Crosscare, Clonliffe College, Dublin 3; www.crosscare.ie; 01-8360011; info@crosscare.ie

DAD.IE

Dad.ie is a parenting website for dads and dads-to-be. It provides parenting advice and information on pregnancy, fatherhood, money, legal issues, and lifestyle and health matters. It is presented in the style of a magazine with articles updated regularly.

www.dad.ie; info@dad.ie

DEPARTMENT OF CHILDREN AND YOUTH AFFAIRS

The Department of Children and Youth Affairs (DCYA) was established in 2011 and there is now a Minister for Children and Youth Affairs. The Department of Children aims to lead the development of a harmonised policy and quality integrated service delivery for children and young people and to carry out specific functions in the social care field and drive coordinated actions across a range of sectors, including health, education, youth justice, sport, arts and culture. It states that the presence of a Minister for Children and Youth Affairs at the Cabinet table will facilitate the development of a seamless approach to the delivery of services to Irish children and that children now have a stronger voice on issues that affect them through the new Ministry.

Department of Children and Youth Affairs, 43-49 Mespil Road, Dublin 4; www.dcya.ie; 01-6473000; omc@dcya.gov.ie

DEPARTMENT OF EDUCATION AND SKILLS

The mission of the Department of Education and Skills is to provide high-quality education which will enable individuals to achieve their full potential and to participate fully as members of society and contribute to Ireland's social, cultural and economic development. The Department's priorities are the promotion of equity and inclusion; quality outcomes and lifelong learning; planning for education that is relevant to personal, social, cultural and economic needs; and enhancement of the capacity of the Department for service delivery, policy formulation, research and evaluation.

www.education.ie

DEPARTMENT OF JUSTICE AND EQUALITY

The mission of the Department of Justice and Equality is to help make Ireland a safer and fairer place in which to live and work, visit and do business. The remit of the Justice family of agencies and services stretches across a range of human concerns and touches on aspects of national life as diverse as the protection of life and property, the prevention and detection of crime, the provision of services for the buying and selling of property, the management of inward migration to the state, and providing the Courts Service and other forms of investigative tribunals. On the international front, the Minister and the Department serve the interests of Ireland in relation to justice and home affairs matters by participating fully in the European Union, the Council of Europe and the United Nations among other international forums.

www.justice.ie; 01-6028202, LoCall 1890-221227; info@ justice.ie

DEPARTMENT OF SOCIAL PROTECTION

The mission of the Department of Social Protection is to promote active participation in society through the provision of income supports, employment services and other services. Its main functions are to advise government and formulate appropriate social protection policies; design, develop and deliver effective and cost-efficient income supports, activation and employment services, advice to customers and other related services; and work towards seamless service delivery in conjunction with other departments, agencies and bodies in the delivery of government policies. The Department plays a

key role in supporting those most in need, including children and their parents, people who are unemployed and ill, people with disabilities and the elderly. Each week approximately 1.4 million people receive a social welfare payment and, when qualified adults and children are included, a total of almost 2.1 million people benefit from weekly payments.
www.welfare.ie

DRUG TREATMENT CENTRE BOARD

The National Drug Advisory and Treatment Centre, now known as the Drug Treatment Centre Board (DTCB), was established in 1969 and is the longest established treatment service in the country. It provides effective, high quality and client-focused treatment in a caring, professional manner in an atmosphere cognisant of the varied individual needs of the client population. It offers guidance and training to other professionals working in the area of substance misuse and contributes to policy development in drug and addiction management. The DTCB is represented on the National Drugs Strategy Committee and the National Advisory Committee on Drugs.
The Drug Treatment Centre Board, McCarthy Centre, 30–31 Pearse Street, Dublin 2; www.addictionireland.ie; 01-6488600; info@dtcb.ie

DUBLIN KIDS

Dublinkids.ie is a children's event and activity guide for Dublin parents, showing the capital city's child-friendly side. It includes events such as family fairs, festivals and art workshops and ongoing attractions such as Dublin

Zoo, the National Aquatic Centre and the city's parks, gardens and more.
dublinkids.ie; 01-8283449

DUBLIN RAPE CRISIS CENTRE

The Dublin Rape Crisis Centre was established in 1979 and is a national organisation offering a wide range of services to women and men who are affected by rape, sexual assault, sexual harassment or childhood sexual abuse. The services include a national 24-hour helpline, training and education, one-to-one counselling, accompaniment to the Sexual Assault Treatment Unit, court accompaniment, campaigning, lobbying and awareness raising, free legal services, and research and statistics. It takes calls from women and men of all ages who have experienced or want to talk about the effects of any kind of sexual violence.
The Dublin Rape Crisis Centre, 70 Lower Leeson Street, Dublin 2; www.drcc.ie; 01-6614911, Freephone 1800-778888; rcc@indigo.ie

EMPOWERING YOUNG PEOPLE IN CARE IN IRELAND

EPIC, formally IAYPIC (the Irish Association of Young People in Care), is an independent association that works throughout Ireland with and for children and young people who are currently living in care or who have had an experience of living in care. This includes those in residential care, foster care, hostels, and high support and special care. It also works with young people preparing to leave care and in aftercare. EPIC was set up to give a voice to young people in care, explain the rights of young people in care, to give information, advice and support to young people with care experience and to help people who work with young people in care to involve them when decisions are being made that relate to them.

EPIC, 7 Red Cow Lane, Smithfield, Dublin 7; www.epiconline. ie; 01-8727661, 087-9036598 (for text messages); info@ epiconline.ie

ENABLE IRELAND

Enable Ireland provides free services to children and adults with disabilities and their families from 40 locations in 14 counties. Its expert teams work with the individuals and their families on a plan for each life stage. Its services for children and their families cover all aspects of a child's physical, educational and social development from early infancy through adolescence. For adults they offer a range of services covering personal development, independent living, supported employment, and social and leisure activities.

Enable Ireland Organisation, Head Office, 32F Rosemount Park Drive, Rosemount Business Park, Ballycoolin Road, Dublin 11; www.enableireland.ie; 01-8727155; communications@enableireland.ie

ENTERTAINING THE KIDS

Entertaining the Kids is a website guide to activities for children in Ireland.

entertainingthekids.ie

EXCHANGE HOUSE NATIONAL TRAVELLERS SERVICE

Exchange House National Travellers Service was established in 1980 at the petition of the Eastern Health Board with the aim of providing family support to the Traveller community in the greater Dublin area. Since then the organisation has developed and is now an organisation of Travellers and settled people working together to provide frontline family support services, addiction services, youth work, educational services, community development, and research and policy to the Traveller community in the greater Dublin area.

Exchange House National Travellers Service, 61 Great Strand Street, Dublin 1; www.exchangehouse.ie; 01-8721094; info@ exchangehouse.ie

FAMILY DIVERSITY INITIATIVE

Family Diversity Initiative is a coalition of organisations working with and representing the interests of diverse families in Ireland. The coalition recognises that the Irish family exists in many different structures and circumstances. Its mission is to promote equality, acceptance and understanding of all family types in Ireland.

Family Diversity Initiative, c/o One Family, Cherish House, 2 Lower Pembroke Street, Dublin 2; www.familydiversity.ie; info@familydiversity.ie

FAMILY LAWYERS ASSOCIATION

The Family Lawyers Association is made up of solicitors and barristers who practise in the area of family law and has hundreds of members spread throughout Ireland. Associate membership is available to other professional persons whose work is connected with family law. The association has been in existence for over twenty years and has served the dual function of promoting contact between family lawyers and fostering a greater level of knowledge and information in regard to family law. *www.familylawyers.ie*

FAMILY MEDIATION SERVICE

The Family Mediation Service is a service to help married and non-married couples who have decided to separate or divorce, or who have already separated. Couples are helped by a mediator to negotiate their own terms of agreement, taking into account the needs and interests of all involved. Is is state-run and staffed by professionally trained and accredited mediators. It was set up in 1986 and has sixteen offices located around the country. It was provided by the Family Support Agency but has been transferred to the Legal Aid Board. *www.fsa.ie, www.legalaidboard.ie*

FAMILY SUPPORT AGENCY

The Family Support Agency is a government agency operating under the Department of Community, Equality and Gaeltacht Affairs. It was set up to provide support to families. It funds 107 family resource centres around Ireland, supports organisations providing marriage, relationship, child and bereavement counselling, researches issues relevant to families, provides information important to families particularly in relation to parenting and advises the Minister for Social Protection on family-related matters.
Family Support Agency, Fourth Floor, St Stephen's Green House, Earlsfort Terrace, Dublin 2; www.fsa.ie; 01-6114100; info@fsa.ie

FAMILY THERAPY ASSOCIATION OF IRELAND

The FTAI is a professional organisation that represents family therapy and therapists in Ireland. It connects those who seek the professional services of a family therapist with qualified, experienced and practicing therapists. The FTAI is a registering body, with a code of ethics that sets professional standards in order to encourage and maintain best practice among therapists and provide clients and patients with the confidence and reassurance that their therapist is well-trained and experienced.
Family Therapy Association of Ireland, 73 Quinn's Road, Shankill, Co. Dublin; www.familytherapyireland.com; 01-2722105

FOCUS IRELAND

Focus Ireland is a registered charity that works to prevent people becoming, remaining or returning to homelessness. The organisation was founded in 1985 by Sr Stanislaus Kennedy in response to the needs of a group of homeless women. Focus Ireland's vision is that 'everyone has a right to a place they can call home' and the organisation works to make this vision a reality for thousands of people every year. Focus Ireland offer services to people in Dublin, Cork, Waterford, Limerick, Sligo and Kilkenny. Its model of housing and services provision focuses on three key areas: prevention, homeless support and housing support. *www.focusireland.ie; Dublin office 01-8815900*

FREE LEGAL ADVICE CENTRES

FLAC is an independent human rights organisation dedicated to the realisation of equal access to justice for all.

To this end it campaigns on a range of legal issues and offers some basic free legal services to the public. FLAC currently concentrates its work on four main areas: legal aid, social welfare, credit and debt, and public interest law. It has centres all over the country.
Free Legal Advice Centres, 13 Lower Dorset Street, Dublin 1; www.flac.ie; 01-874569, LoCall 1890-350250

GAMBLERS ANONYMOUS

Gamblers Anonymous (GA) is a fellowship of men and women who share their experience, strength and hope with each other that they may solve their common problem and help others to recover from a gambling problem. The only requirement for membership is a desire to stop gambling. There are no dues or fees for GA membership. It is self-supporting through its own contributions. GA is not allied with any sect, denomination, politics, organisation or institution.
Gamblers Anonymous, Carmichael House, North Brunswick Street, Dublin 7/Quaker House, Capwell, Summerhill South, Cork City; www.gamblersanonymous.ie; Dublin 01-8721133, Cork 087-2859552, Galway 086-3494450, Waterford 086-2683538, 086-3973317; info@gamblersanonymous.ie

GAY AND LESBIAN EQUALITY NETWORK

GLEN is a non-governmental organisation that works to achieve full equality and inclusion for lesbian, gay and bisexual (LGB) people in Ireland and to protect them from all forms of discrimination. GLEN believes that high ambitions are necessary in order to achieve high quality outcomes and is committed to delivering ambitious change both for our communities and for Ireland. It is working to achieve a future in which LGB people can make an even more creative and dynamic contribution to the social, economic and cultural development of Ireland. *GLEN, 2 Exchange Street Upper, Dublin 8; www.glen.ie; 01-6728650; info@glen.ie*

GROW

GROW is a mental health organisation that helps people who have suffered, or are suffering, from mental health problems. Members are helped to recover from all forms of mental breakdown or to prevent a breakdown happening. It was founded in Australia in 1957 by former mental illness sufferers and has a national network of over 130 groups in Ireland. Its principal strength is the support members give each other from their own experiences in matters to do with mental health.
www.grow.ie; 1890-474474; info@grow.ie

HEADSTRONG

Headstrong is the National Centre for Youth Mental Health, a non-profit organisation supporting young people's mental health in Ireland. It has four main areas of activity: service development, advocacy, research and evaluation. Its service development programme, Jigsaw, brings community services and supports together around young people in order to better meet their mental health needs. It advocates at a national and local level for the right of young people to access better mental health supports, and a change in the way Ireland thinks about youth mental health.
Headstrong, the National Centre for Youth Mental Health, 16 Westland Square, Pearse Street, Dublin 2; www.headstrong.ie; 01-4727010; info@headstrong.ie

HEALTH SERVICE EXECUTIVE

The Health Service Executive delivers thousands of different health and social services in hospitals and communities across the country, 24 hours a day. Its website helps customers find the services they need and gives details and locations of all its services, news and information, and publications.
www.hse.ie; 1850-241850

IMMIGRANT COUNCIL OF IRELAND

The Immigrant Council of Ireland (ICI) was established by Sr Stanislaus Kennedy in 2001. In its organisation migrants and Irish people work together to provide information, support and legal advice to immigrants and their families. Two important principles underpin their work: that immigration is a permanent and positive reality in Ireland and that individuals' human rights must be respected, protected and upheld. It also has an independent law centre and lobbies for integrated, transparent, rights-based immigration and integration legislation and policies which reflect this reality.
ICI, 2 St Andrew Street, Dublin 2; www.immigrantcouncil.ie; 01-6740200, 01-6740202; info@immigrantcouncil.ie

INCLUSION IRELAND

The vision of Inclusion Ireland is that of people with intellectual disabilities living and participating in the community with equal rights as citizens, able to live the life of their choice to their fullest potential. It provides a central forum for its members to identify priorities and formulate nationally agreed policies to present to

government, statutory bodies and other relevant groups as well as the general public.
Inclusion Ireland, Unit C2, The Steelworks, Foley St, Dublin 1; www.inclusionireland.ie; 01-8559891; info@ inclusionireland.ie

INSPIRE IRELAND FOUNDATION

Inspire Ireland Foundation is a charitable organisation that helps young people lead happier lives. It is part of an international network of foundations with the same mission, operating in Australia and the US. It achieves its mission through the delivery of ReachOut.com, an online service to help young people aged 16–25 get through tough times. It was established in Australia in 1996 in direct response to Australia's then escalating rates of youth suicide. Combining technology with the direct involvement of young people it delivers an innovative and practical online programme that helps prevent youth suicide and improves young people's mental health and wellbeing.
Inspire Ireland Foundation, First Floor, 29–31 South William Street, Dublin 2; www.inspireireland.ie, ReachOut.com; 01-7645666

INSTITUTE OF COGNITIVE BEHAVIOURAL THERAPY

The Institute of Cognitive Behavioural Therapy (ICBT) is a professional organisation of cognitive behavioural therapists. Its major objective is to make cognitive behavioural therapy more readily available throughout the country by training therapists to high levels of competence. It also promotes education among health professionals and the general public regarding the causes of emotional and behavioural problems. The institute consists mainly

of therapists who have trained in the Rational Emotive Behaviour Therapy modality of CBT.
Institute of Cognitive Behavioural Therapy, 91 Balreask Manor, Trim Road, Navan, Co. Meath; www.icbt.ie

IRISH ASSOCIATION FOR COUNSELLING AND PSYCHOTHERAPY

The Irish Association for Counselling and Psychotherapy (IACP) was established in 1981. It identifies, develops and maintains professional standards of excellence in counselling and psychotherapy through education, training and accreditation. It promotes best practice and the professional development of its members and holds at its core the protection of the public. It represents both the interests of clients and over 3,500 practitioners nationwide, provides a telephone referral helpline, an information service and an online counsellor, psychotherapist and supervisor director. It acts as a link between those who are looking for counselling or psychotherapy and those who provide counselling or psychotherapy.
Irish Association for Counselling and Psychotherapy, 21 Dublin Road, Bray, Co. Wicklow; www.irish-counselling.ie; 01-2723427; iacp@iacp.ie

IRISH ASSOCIATION OF HUMANISTIC AND INTEGRATIVE PSYCHOTHERAPY

The Irish Association of Humanistic and Integrative Psychotherapy (IAHIP) was formed in 1992 as an association to represent humanistic and integrative psychotherapists in Ireland. It acts as the professional body in Ireland for humanistic and integrative psychotherapy and sets and maintains standards of training and practice. It keeps a register of all accredited practitioners, promotes the provision of training and education, and undertakes and encourages research in theory and practice.

Irish Association of Humanistic and Integrative Psychotherapy, 44 Northumberland Avenue, Dun Laoghaire, Co. Dublin; www.iahip.com; 01-2841665; info@iahip.org

IRISH CENTRE FOR PARENTALLY ABDUCTED CHILDREN

The ICPAC is a telephone helpline for parents whose children have been abducted or who fear abduction.

01-6620667; icpacseminar@gmail.com

IRISH COLLEGE OF GENERAL PRACTITIONERS

The Irish College of General Practitioners (ICGP) is the professional body for doctors in general practice in Ireland. Its primary aim is to serve patients and general practitioners by encouraging and maintaining the highest standards of general medical practice. It is the representative organisation for education, training and standards in general practice and is the recognised body for the accreditation of specialist training in general practice in Ireland. It is recognised by the Irish Medical Council as the representative academic body for the specialty of general practice. At an international level the College is a member of the World Organisation of National Colleges and Academies and Academic Associations of General Practice (WONCA). Its website will help patients find a GP is their local area.

ICGP, 4/5 Lincoln Place, Dublin 2; www.icgp.ie; 01-6763705; info@icgp.ie

IRISH COUNCIL FOR CIVIL LIBERTIES

The Irish Council for Civil Liberties (ICCL) is Ireland's leading independent human rights watchdog. It monitors, educates and campaigns in order to secure full enjoyment of human rights for everyone. It has played a leading role in some of Ireland's most successful human rights campaigns. These have included campaigns to establish an independent Garda Ombudsman Commission, legalise the right to divorce, secure more effective protection of children's rights, decriminalise homosexuality and introduce enhanced equality legislation.
ICCL, 9–13 Blackhall Place, Dublin 7; www.iccl.ie; 01-7994504; info@iccl.ie

IRISH COUNCIL FOR PSYCHOTHERAPY

The primary aim of the Irish Council for Psychotherapy is to serve clients, patients and psychotherapists by encouraging and maintaining the highest standards of practice. It believes that when a person is seeking the services of a psychotherapist it is important to find someone who is experienced and well trained. It acts as a link between those who are looking for psychotherapeutic services and those who provide psychotherapeutic services and its website can be used to find a psychotherapist.
ICP, 13 Farnogue Park, Wexford; www.psychotherapy-ireland. com; 01-9023819

IRISH FAMILY PLANNING ASSOCIATION

The Irish Family Planning Association (IFPA) is Ireland's leading sexual health charity. The organisation promotes the right of all people to sexual and reproductive health information and dedicated, confidential and affordable healthcare services. It was established by seven volunteers in 1969. Since then it has been to the fore in setting the agenda for sexual and reproductive health and rights both nationally and internationally. It offers a comprehensive range of services which promote sexual health and support reproductive choice on a not-for-profit basis. It has a pregnancy counselling service, an education and training service, and is involved in advocacy and raising awareness.

IFPA, Solomons House, 42a Pearse Street, Dublin 2; www. ifpa.ie; 01-6074456; National Pregnancy Helpline 1850-495051; post@ifpa.ie

IRISH MEDICAL COUNCIL

The Irish Medical Council (IMC) regulates doctors to practise medicine in the Republic of Ireland. Its statutory role, as outlined in the Medical Practitioners Act 2007, is to protect the public by promoting and better ensuring high standards of professional education, training and competence among registered practitioners. The key responsibilities of the IMC include maintaining the Register of Medical Practitioners, a register of all medical practitioners legally entitled to work in Ireland; ensuring high standards of medical education and training; setting high standards for the maintenance of professional competence; promoting good medical practice; and investigating complaints against medical practitioners.

IMO, Kingram House, Kingram Place, Dublin 2; www. medicalcouncil.ie; 01-4983100; info@mcirl.ie

IRISH NATIONAL ORGANISATION OF THE UNEMPLOYED

The Irish National Organisation of the Unemployed (INOU) is a federation of unemployed people, unemployed centres, unemployed groups, community organisations and trade unions. It represents and defends the rights and interests of those who want decent employment and cannot obtain it. It also campaigns for an acceptable standard of living for unemployed people and their dependents. The INOU is an anti-sectarian, anti-racist, non-party political organisation which promotes equality of opportunity within society.

INOU, Araby House, 8 North Richmond Street, Dublin 1; www.inou.ie; 01-8560088; info@inou.ie

IRISH REFUGEE COUNCIL

The Irish Refugee Council (IRC) is Ireland's only national non-governmental organisation which specialises in working with and for refugees in Ireland. The main focus of its work is on those in the asylum system who are applying to be recognised as refugees. For almost twenty years it has observed the changes that have been made in response to the arrival of refugees in Ireland. Based on extensive experience working directly with those affected, it has seen the huge financial cost of a failed system and the untold damage that has and is being done to men, women and children in the asylum process. The IRC is committed to promoting an asylum system that will be beneficial for refugees, the decision maker and the taxpayer.

IRC, Second Floor, Ballast House, Aston Quay, Dublin 2; www.irishrefugeecouncil.ie; 01-7645854; info@ irishrefugeecouncil.ie

IRISH SOCIETY FOR THE PREVENTION OF CRUELTY TO CHILDREN

The ISPCC was founded in 1889. Its aims are to ensure that all children are heard and valued. It operates Child-line, which is a 24-hour listening service for children, Leanbh, which is a 24-hour service that works with children who are begging on the streets of Dublin, a mentoring service and a behavioural and emotional support service for children.

ISPCC Head Office, 29 Lower Baggot Street, Dublin 2; www. ispcc.ie

IRISH TRAVELLER MOVEMENT

The Irish Traveller Movement (ITM) is a national network of organisations and individuals working within the Traveller community. It was established in 1990 and now has over 80 Traveller organisations from all parts of Ireland in its membership. It consists of a partnership between Travellers and settled people committed to seeking full equality for Travellers in Irish society. It seeks real solutions, debates ideas and formulates and promotes culturally appropriate initiatives, provides those active at a local level with support and solidarity, develops alliances at national level and challenges the many forms of individual, structural and institutional racism with which Travellers have to deal.

ITM, 4/5 Eustace Street, Dublin 2; www.itmtrav.ie; 01-6796577; itmtrav@indigo.ie

IRISH YOUTH FOUNDATION

The mission of the Irish Youth Foundation (IYF) is to provide opportunities for children and young people facing adverse and extreme conditions to experience success in their lives. Whenever possible the IYF seeks to address the underlying causes of poverty, educational disadvantage, homelessness and social exclusion experienced by children and young people.

IYF, Second Floor, 56 Fitzwilliam Square, Dublin 2; www.iyf. ie; 01-6766535; info@iyf.ie

LAW REFORM COMMISSION

The Law Reform Commission is an independent body established under the Law Reform Commission Act 1975. Its purpose is to keep the law under review and make recommendations for law reform so that the law reflects the changing needs of Irish society. Since it was established it has published over 160 documents containing proposals for law reform. It has a very useful legislation and publications library on its website.

Law Reform Commission, 35–39 Shelbourne Road, Ballsbridge, Dublin 4; www.lawreform.ie; 01-6377600; info@lawreform.ie

LAW SOCIETY OF IRELAND

The Law Society of Ireland is the educational, representative and regulatory body of the solicitors' profession in Ireland. It exercises statutory functions under the Solicitors Acts 1954–2008 in relation to the education, admission, enrolment, discipline and regulation of the solicitors' profession. It is the professional body for its 12,000 solicitor members, to whom it also provides services and support. Its website has a search facility for finding solicitors around the country and a complaints procedure section.

Law Society of Ireland, Blackhall Place, Dublin 7; www.lawsociety.ie; 01-6724800; general@lawsociety.ie

LEGAL AID BOARD

The Legal Aid Board is an independent, publicly funded organisation. It has been in existence since 1979 and was set up as a statutory body on foot of the Civil Legal Aid Act 1995. The Board's mission statement is 'To provide a professional, efficient, cost-effective and accessible legal aid and advice service' and it provides subsidised legal services to people who cannot afford representation in court. It has 33 full-time law centres located throughout the country, as well as a private practitioner service, a refugee documentation centre and a library service located at Montague Court, Montague Lane, Dublin 2. It also has responsibility for the administration of the Family Mediation Service and the Garda Station Legal Advice Scheme.
Legal Aid Board, Quay Street, Cahirciveen, Co. Kerry/47 Upper Mount Street, Dublin 2; www.legalaidboard.ie; Head office 066-9471000, LoCall 1890-615200, Dublin office 01-6441900; info@legalaidboard.ie

MEDIATORS' INSTITUTE OF IRELAND

The Mediators' Institute of Ireland (MII) is the professional association for mediators in the Republic of Ireland and Northern Ireland. It was established in 1992 and it promotes the use and practice of quality mediation as a process of dispute resolution. Members adhere to a code of ethics and are required to have professional indemnity insurance. It has clear and transparent accreditation, training and continuing professional development requirements that meet international and professional standards. Its website provides information on mediation and how to find a mediator.
MII, 35 Fitzwilliam Place, Dublin 2; www.themii.ie; 01-6099190; info@themii.ie

MENTAL HEALTH COMMISSION

The Mental Health Commission is an independent statutory body established under the Mental Health Act 2001. It works to promote high standards in the delivery of mental health services and ensures the interests of those involuntarily admitted to approved centres are protected and the patients are given legal representation. Its website gives information on mental health tribunals, the registration of approved centres, standards and quality assurance, and training and development.

Mental Health Commission, St Martin's House, Waterloo Road, Dublin 4; www.mhcirl.ie; 01-6362400; info@mhcirl.ie

MENTAL HEALTH IRELAND

Mental Health Ireland aims to promote positive mental health and to actively support people with mental illnesses and their families and carers by identifying their needs and advocating for their rights. It supports local mental health associations in their work, campaigning and advocating to improve national mental health policy and service provision, providing an information service on issues relating to mental health, undertaking research on mental health topics, such as the national survey on stress and the national survey on public attitudes to mental illness, and organising conferences, courses, workshops and seminars on a wide variety of issues relating to mental health. MHI also promotes and coordinates activities to celebrate World Mental Health Day on 10 October each year.

Mental Health Ireland, Head Office, Mensana House, 6 Adelaide Street, Dun Laoghaire, Co. Dublin; www. mentalhealthireland.ie; 01-2841166; info@mentalhealthireland. ie

MERCHANTS QUAY IRELAND

Merchants Quay Ireland's vision is of a society where nobody is without a place to call home and where the incidence of drug-related harm is greatly reduced and the range and quality of drugs services are maximised. Its mission is to provide services aimed at reducing harm related to drug use and homelessness and at providing pathways towards rehabilitation and settlement, and to work for positive social change to combat poverty and social exclusion. It provides services and treatment for drug users, including homelessness services, settlement and integration services, residential drug treatment, and training and research.

MQI, Head Office, 28 Winetavern St, Dublin 8; www.mqi.ie; 01-5240160; info@mqi.ie

MONEY ADVICE AND BUDGETING SERVICE

The Money Advice and Budgeting Service (MABS) is a national free, confidential, independent and non-judgemental service for people in debt or in danger of getting into debt. It has a helpline and gives advice on money management and dealing with debt. It helps people assess their situation, make payments and manage their money. It has local offices around the country. MABS works with clients by supporting them in drawing up realistic budgets and maximising their incomes. MABS also supports clients in dealing with their debts according to their budgets. MABS does not give financial advice or advice on investments or on specific financial products. MABS also does not give out money.

www.mabs.ie; 0761-072000; helpline@mabs.ie

NARCOTICS ANONYMOUS

Narcotics Anonymous (NA) is a non-profit fellowship of men and women for whom drugs has become a major problem. It is run by recovering addicts who meet regularly to help each other stay clean. The information on its website is provided for those who think they may have a drug problem, professionals working with addicts seeking recovery and NA members. It has a meeting list where addicts can find NA meetings in Ireland.

Narcotics Anonymous Ireland, Irish Regional Service Committee, 29 Bride Street, Dublin 8; www.na-ireland.org; 01-6728000; info@na-ireland.org

NATIONAL DISABILITY AUTHORITY

The National Disability Authority is the lead state agency on disability issues, providing independent expert advice to government on policy and practice and promoting universal design in Ireland. It strives to ensure that the rights and entitlements of people with disabilities are protected. It acts as a national body to assist in the coordination and development of disability policy; undertakes research and develops statistical information for planning; delivers and monitors programmes and services for people with disabilities; advises the Minister for Disability, Equality and Mental Health on standards for programmes and services; prepares codes of practice; monitors the implementation of standards and codes of practice; and takes the lead in both encouraging and recognising the promotion of equality of people with disabilities.

NDA, 25 Clyde Road, Dublin 4; www.nda.ie; 01-6080400; nda@nda.ie

OMBUDSMAN FOR CHILDREN'S OFFICE

The Ombudsman for Children's Office (OCO) aims to make sure that the government and other people who make decisions about young people really think about what is best for young people. Its powers are set out in the Ombudsman for Children Act 2002. Its main areas of work are independent complaints handling, communication and participation, research and policy. Its work is to support people, including children and young people; to find out more about children's and young people's rights; to find out what's important to young people and let the government and others know what matters to young people themselves; to carry out research to get a better understanding of things that are really important in children's and young people's lives; to give advice to the government and others about doing what's best for children and young people; and to receive and, where possible, look into complaints made by young people or by adults on young people's behalf.
The Ombudsman for Children's Office, Millennium House, 52–56 Great Strand Street, Dublin 1; www.oco.ie; 01-8656800, Freephone 1800-202040; oco@oco.ie

ONE FAMILY

One Family is a leading national organisation for one-parent families in Ireland. It works with all types and all members of one-parent families, respecting the realities of family life in Ireland, to affect positive change and achieve equality and social inclusion for all one-parent families in Ireland. It aims to provide high quality, much needed services to the many different one-parent families in Ireland and the professionals working with them. It also works hard to ensure that one-parent families have a clear voice that is heard by policy and decision makers. It has a childcare service, parenting mentoring, positive parenting courses, family communication courses and counselling services.

One Family, 2 Lower Pembroke Street, Dublin 2; www. onefamily.ie; 01-6629212, LoCall 1890-662212; info@one family.ie

ONE IN FOUR

One in Four offers a voice to and support for women and men who have experienced sexual abuse and/or sexual violence and also to their family and friends. Support is provided directly through individual psychotherapy, group therapy, advocacy/support, and 24-hour support on our online message boards. One in Four liaises with both statutory and non-statutory agencies, where necessary, such as child protection agencies, An Garda Síochána and other agencies that may offer further support and assistance to the family.

One in Four, 2 Holles Street, Dublin 2; www.oneinfour.org; 01-6624070; info@oneinfour.org

PACT

Pact is a small independent Irish charity founded in 1952 as an adoption agency. Today it provides a broad range of services in the area of adoption, information and tracing, and unplanned pregnancy. Its name symbolises an agreement made between two parties. Its aim is to build a relationship with clients, based on mutual trust, and to provide a caring, professional service. It offers a comprehensive crisis pregnancy and adoption service and

provides a continuum of care for all its clients. Its service is free of charge and non-medical only.
PACT, Arabella House, 18D Nutgrove Office Park, Rathfarn-ham, Dublin 14; www.pact.ie; 01-2962200, Crisis Pregnancy Line 1850-673333; info@pact.ie

PARENTLINE

Parentline has provided a completely confidential helpline for parents and guardians for over twenty years. There is no typical call. Calls come from parents of newborn babies, toddlers, pre-teens and teenagers – children of all ages. All ages offer different challenges. It offers support, guidance and information on all aspects of being a parent and the reassurance that, whatever the problem, you're not the first parent to face it. All its facilitators receive extensive training before going on the lines.
Parentline, Carmichael Centre, North Brunswick St, Dublin 7; www.parentline.ie; 1890-927277, 01-8733500; info@ parentline.ie

PAVEE POINT

Pavee Point is a voluntary non-governmental organisation committed to the attainment of human rights for Irish Trav-ellers. The group is comprised of Travellers and members of the majority population working together in partner-ship to address the needs of Travellers as a minority group experiencing exclusion and marginalisation. Its aim is to contribute to improvement in the quality of life and living circumstances of Irish Travellers, through working for social justice, solidarity, socio-economic development and human rights.

Pavee Point Travellers' Centre, 46 North Great Charles Street, Dublin 1; www.paveepoint.ie; 01-8780255; info@ pavee.ie

PENSIONS BOARD

The Pensions Board is a statutory body set up under the Pensions Act 1990. It regulates occupational pension schemes, trust RAC schemes and personal retirement savings accounts in Ireland. It mission is to support a sustainable pensions system that will provide adequate and reliable pensions for retired and older people and that achieves wide coverage. It aims to achieve this by safeguarding pensions through regulation, providing information and guidance, and developing policy and proposals.

The Pensions Board, Verschoyle House, 28–30 Lower Mount Street, Dublin 2; www.pensionsboard.ie; 01-6131900, LoCall 1890-656565; info@pensionsboard.ie

PSYCHOLOGICAL SOCIETY OF IRELAND

The Psychological Society of Ireland (PSI) is the professional body for the psychological profession in Ireland, with the primary object of advancing psychology as a pure and applied science in Ireland and elsewhere. The PSI strives to promote quality psychological practice and foster learning and growth, by setting high standards of professional education and conduct.

PSI, Floor 2, Grantham House, Grantham Street, Dublin 2; www.psihq.ie; 01-4720105; info@psihq.ie

RAPE CRISIS CENTRE – see DUBLIN RAPE CRISIS CENTRE

RELATIONSHIPS IRELAND

Relationships Ireland, formerly the Marriage and Relationship Counselling Services, was founded in 1962 and is one of Ireland's leading counselling agencies providing services to those with problems in their personal relationships. It is a registered charity and is governed by a board of directors. Its services include relationship counselling, therapy for individuals and couples experiencing sexual problems, marriage preparation courses, relationship breakdown and separation counselling, training for professionals, affordable courses for the public and a counselling service for teenagers.

Relationships Ireland, 38 Upper Fitzwilliam Street, Dublin 2; www.relationshipsireland.com; 01-6785256, LoCall 1890-380380; info@relationshipsireland.com

SAMARITANS

The Samaritans provides confidential non-judgemental emotional support, 24 hours a day, for people who are experiencing feelings of distress or despair, including those which could lead to suicide. It is not a religious or a political organisation, doesn't make judgements or offer advice. Instead, it believes in the value of having time and space to explore difficult feelings. It believes that being listened to in confidence and accepted without prejudice can alleviate despair and suicidal feelings. It offers its service by telephone, email, letter and face-to-face meetings in most of its branches. It provides courses to businesses to help staff and teaching programmes for schools and prisons.

Samaritans, 112 Marlborough Street, Dublin 1; www. samaritans.org; 1850-609090; jo@samaritans.org

SOCIETY OF ST VINCENT DE PAUL

The Society of St Vincent de Paul is the largest voluntary charitable organisation in Ireland. It has a membership of 9,500 volunteers throughout the country, supported by professional staff, working for social justice and the creation of a more just, caring nation. The aim of the St Vincent de Paul Society is to tackle poverty in all its forms through the provision of practical assistance to those in need.

National Office, SVP House, 91–92 Sean MacDermott Street, Dublin 1; www.svp.ie; 01-8386990; info@svp.ie

STOP IT NOW!

Stop It Now! UK and Ireland is a campaign managed by the Lucy Faithfull Foundation which aims to prevent child sexual abuse by raising awareness and encouraging early recognition and responses to the problem by abusers themselves and those close to them. It believes that sexual abuse is preventable and urges abusers and potential abusers to seek help and gives adults the information they need to protect children effectively. It encourages adults to create a society that no longer tolerates the sexual abuse of children.

Stop It Now, Lord Bordesley Hall, The Holloway, Alvechurch, Birmingham B48 7QA, UK; www.stopitnow.org; +353 152-7598184; office@stopitnow.org.uk, for confidential emails: help@stopitnow.org.uk

TEEN BETWEEN

Teen Between is a specialised counselling service which supports teenagers with separated or divorced parents. The service was set up fourteen years ago out of a need identified by parents in counselling with MRCS (Marriage and Relationship Counselling Services). Since its inception Teen Between has aimed to give teenagers struggling with parental separation the tools to maintain a healthy relationship with both parents, while also coping with the additional struggles of entering adulthood. It aims to give these teenagers a sense of partnership and belonging both within the family unit and within society, something so important during this time of transition. Teen Between is also delivered in over 40 locations around the country in a partnership programme with Youth Work Ireland.

Teen Between, 38 Upper Fitzwilliam Street, Dublin 2; www.relationshipsireland.ie, teenbetween.ie; 1890-303191; teenbetween@mrcs.ie

THRESHOLD

Threshold is a registered charity founded in 1978. Its aim is to secure a right to housing, particularly for households experiencing the problems of poverty and exclusion. It does this by campaigning, analysing the existing problems, providing independent advice and advocacy, and working in collaboration with those disadvantaged by the housing system. It has advice centres in Dublin, Galway and Cork.

Threshold, 21 Stoneybatter, Dublin 7; www.threshold.ie; 01-6786096; advice@threshold.ie, thresholdgalway@eircom. net, advicecork@threshold.ie

TREOIR

Treoir is the national information centre for unmarried parents. It aims to provide accurate, confidential and free information to parents who are not married to each other and to those involved with them, including grandparents. It provides information on birth registration, establishing paternity, access, custody, guardianship, maintenance and social welfare entitlements. It has an online information pack, offers workshops around the country on different issues, produces a wide range of publications, promotes the rights and interests of unmarried parents, commissions research, and regularly networks with other agencies. *Treoir, 14 Gandon House, Lower Mayor Street, IFSC, Dublin 1; www.treoir.ie; 01-6700120, LoCall 1890-252084; info@ treoir.ie*

UNITED NATIONS INTERNATIONAL CHILDREN'S EMERGENCY RELIEF FUND

UNICEF was founded by the UN General Assembly in 1946. UNICEF Ireland saves and protects the lives of children by supporting UNICEF's work through fundraising, advocacy and education in Ireland. Working in over 150 countries across the world, UNICEF is committed to finding the best and most cost-effective ways to save children's lives, providing healthcare, nutrition and education to help every child realise their full potential. UNICEF Ireland also advocates for lasting change for children. For example, UNICEF Ireland works to change government policies and practices that are detrimental to children's rights in Ireland and internationally. *UNICEF Ireland, 33 Lower Ormond Quay, Dublin 1; www. unicef.ie; 01-8783000; info@unicef.ie*

WOMEN'S AID

Women's Aid is a leading national organisation that has been working to address the issue of domestic violence in Ireland for more than 35 years. In this time it has built up a huge body of experience and expertise on the issue, enabling it to best support women and share its knowledge with other agencies responding to women experiencing domestic violence. Its direct services to women experiencing domestic violence underpin and inform all its work towards ending violence against women. Women's Aid provides a national Freephone helpline that provides support and information to callers experiencing abuse from intimate partners, one-on-one information and support in locations throughout Dublin and a court accompaniment service. It also provides training and information, works to raise awareness of domestic violence issues, conducts research on domestic violence and seeks to influence legislative change to improve responses to women experiencing domestic violence.

Women's Aid, 5 Wilton Place, Dublin 2; www.womensaid.ie; Freephone 1800-341900, 01-6788858; info@womensaid.ie

YOUTHREACH

Youthreach is a national programme of second chance education and training in Ireland and is a central part of the government's contribution to the achievement of a lifelong learning society. The programme is directed at unemployed young early school leavers aged 15–20 and it offers participants the opportunity to identify and pursue viable options within adult life and provides them with opportunities to acquire certification.

Siobhan McGurk, c/o Curriculum Development Unit, Captain's Road, Dublin 12; www.youthreach.ie; 01-4535487; youthreachinfo@cdu.cdvec.ie